BASIC TEXTS IN COUNSELLING

Series editor: Stephen Frosh

This series introduces readers to the [...] psychotherapy across a wide range of topic areas. The books appeal to anyone wishing to use counselling and psychotherapeutic skills and are particularly relevant to workers in health, education, social work and related settings. The books are unusual in being rooted in psychodynamic and systemic ideas, yet being written at an accessible, readable and introductory level. Each text offers theoretical background and guidance for practice, with creative use of clinical examples.

Published

Jenny Altschuler
WORKING WITH CHRONIC ILLNESS

Bill Barnes, Sheila Ernst and Keith Hyde
AN INTRODUCTION TO GROUPWORK

Stephen Briggs
WORKING WITH ADOLESCENTS AND YOUNG ADULTS 2nd Edition

Alex Coren
SHORT-TERM PSYCHOTHERAPY

Jim Crawley and Jan Grant
COUPLE THERAPY

Emilia Dowling and Gill Gorell Barnes
WORKING WITH CHILDREN AND PARENTS THROUGH SEPARATION AND DIVORCE

Loretta Franklin
AN INTRODUCTION TO WORKPLACE COUNSELLING

Gill Gorell Barnes
FAMILY THERAPY IN CHANGING TIMES 2nd Edition

Fran Hedges
AN INTRODUCTION TO SYSTEMATIC THERAPY WITH INDIVIDUALS

Sally Hodges
COUNSELLING ADULTS WITH LEARNING DISABILITIES

Linda Hopper
COUNSELLING AND PSYCHOTHERAPY WITH CHILDREN AND ADOLESCENTS

Ravi Rana
COUNSELLING STUDENTS

Tricia Scott
INTEGRATIVE PSYCHOTHERAPY IN HEALTHCARE

Geraldine Shipton
WORKING WITH EATING DISORDERS

Laurence Spurling
AN INTRODUCTION TO PSYCHODYNAMIC COUNSELLING 2nd Edition

Paul Terry
COUNSELLING AND PSYCHOTHERAPY WITH OLDER PEOPLE 2nd Edition

Jan Wiener and Mannie Sher
COUNSELLING AND PSYCHOTHERAPY IN PRIMARY HEALTH CARE

Shula Wilson
DISABILITY, COUNSELLING AND PSYCHOTHERAPY

Steven Walker
CULTURALLY COMPETENT THERAPY

Invitation to authors

The Series Editor welcomes proposals for new books within the Basic Texts in Counselling and Psychotherapy series. These should be sent to Stephen Frosh at the School of Psychology, Birkbeck College, Malet Street, London, WC1E 7HX (e-mail s.frosh@bbk.ac.uk)

Basic Texts in Counselling and Psychotherapy
Series Standing Order ISBN 0–333–69330–2
(*outside North America only*)

You can receive future titles in this series as they are published by placing a standing order. Please contact your bookseller or, in the case of difficulty, write to us at the address below with your name and address, the title of the series and the ISBN quoted above.

Customer Services Department, Macmillan Distribution Ltd, Houndmills, Basingstoke, Hampshire RG21 6XS, England

SUPERVISION IN COUNSELLING AND PSYCHOTHERAPY

AN INTRODUCTION

LIZ OMAND

palgrave
macmillan

First published 2009 by
PALGRAVE MACMILLAN

Palgrave Macmillan in the UK is an imprint of Macmillan Publishers Limited,
registered in England, company number 785998, of Houndmills, Basingstoke,
Hampshire RG21 6XS.

Palgrave Macmillan in the US is a division of St Martin's Press LLC,
175 Fifth Avenue, New York, NY 10010.

Palgrave Macmillan is the global academic imprint of the above companies
and has companies and representatives throughout the world.

Palgrave® and Macmillan® are registered trademarks in the United States,
the United Kingdom, Europe and other countries.

ISBN-13: 978–0–230–00632–4

This book is printed on paper suitable for recycling and made from fully
managed and sustained forest sources. Logging, pulping and manufacturing
processes are expected to conform to the environmental regulations of the
country of origin.

A catalogue record for this book is available from the British Library.

A catalog record for this book is available from the Library of Congress.

10   9   8   7   6   5   4   3   2   1
18 17 16 15 14 13 12 11 10 09

Printed and bound in China

For David

CONTENTS

Acknowledgements

In writing this book I have become aware of having drawn on a variety of resources and influences. As this book suggests, supervision is a rich experience involving mutual learning and I would like to thank all my supervisees for their part in my education. Some of them have contributed examples for this book and I am grateful for their generosity in allowing their experiences to be used in this way. My own supervisors have also demonstrated what is involved in good supervision and two in particular, Maggie Cohen and Fakhry Davids, have at different times helped me develop as a supervisor as well as a psychotherapist.

Good supervision might be partly a matter of training, and the beginning of the process of thinking about the subject was stimulated by attending a course in psychodynamic supervision at Leicester University; I benefitted greatly from my contact with the tutors and other students on this course. But the quality of our supervision also reflects the extent to which we have integrated our core theoretical training and understanding with practice and I owe a great deal to all those who were involved in my training, first as a counsellor at Birkbeck, University of London, and later at the British Association of Psychotherapists. My own analysis was of course very important in my development.

More recently, my students and colleagues on the MSc in Psychodynamic Counselling at Birkbeck College have provided a creative and challenging impetus to the development of my understanding. They have taught me a great deal about working in different settings, as has my participation on the group relations conferences which are part of the course. I have also benefitted from my involvement on the supervision course at the BAP and the experience and wisdom of my colleagues and those attending the course.

I am grateful for the help and encouragement of those who gave me their comments on individual chapters of the book, including Jan Baker, Stewart Beever, Ann Heyno, Laurence Spurling and Richard Tan. I would like to thank Paul Terry, who also gave the manuscript a very thorough and constructive consideration. My editor,

Stephen Frosh, has also been very encouraging, and his pertinent comments on the first drafts of the book have been important in its development and completion. Thanks also to Catherine Gray at Palgrave.

Finally, my thanks are due to various members of my family for their forbearance and encouragement, in particular to David to whom this book is dedicated.

Liz Omand

INTRODUCTION

What makes supervision so difficult?

This book is the result of an interest and preoccupation – amounting at times to a struggle – with the subject of supervision. It draws on my experience of supervision over the years. I include in this my experience as a supervisee as well as a supervisor, in a range of counselling and psychotherapy contexts, always within the psychodynamic tradition.

Writing about this subject has allowed me to make sense of my experience; I wanted to explore the dilemmas and paradoxes of being a supervisor. I think that these are not always recognised when we find ourselves beginning to supervise, and we need to find ways of thinking about the complexity of the work without getting overwhelmed by it. It is an activity which many of us find rewarding and deeply satisfying; it provides an opportunity to work with counsellors and therapists at the beginning of their careers, as well as with more experienced colleagues. But supervision can also at times be frustrating and difficult. I know I am not alone in this – conversations with colleagues suggest that we can all find providing supervision a challenge at times. And we all remember times, perhaps in the course of our training, when we felt disheartened by our own supervision.

I imagine therefore that this book will be particularly useful for those who are beginning to supervise; as I suggest in Chapter 2, we can sometimes find ourselves being asked to do this without a great deal of preparation. More experienced practitioners who want the opportunity to think about the dynamics of supervision might also find it useful as an introduction to the subject. Of course, a book can never be a substitute for talking with colleagues or our own supervisor about specific supervisory problems, or for developing supervision skills by attending a course on the subject. But it might provide some help in identifying and thinking about areas of concern. Those receiving supervision – and possibly thinking ahead to possibilities for doing supervision in the future – might also find it helpful, if only in allowing an imaginative identification with the role of supervisor and a different way of thinking about their own supervision. Although the main focus of this book is to do with the supervisor's role, supervision involves a relationship – a supervisor cannot function effectively without a supervisee who is prepared to think about their role and take responsibility for their part in the process of supervision.

The task of supervision is complex. Supervisors are normally experienced therapists, but being in role as a supervisor means using this experience in a different way, to inform our interventions, resisting the temptation to interpret directly. The process is complicated by the fact that the main subject of the discussion is not in the room with us – in psychodynamic supervision we are meeting to think about a third, absent, person, the client or patient. When Zinkin (1988) wrote of supervision as the 'impossible profession' he was thinking partly of the difficulty for the supervisee of conveying, and for the supervisor of understanding, something of what has gone on in this other setting.

This three-person relationship is also reflected in the idea to which many writers draw attention, of the role of the supervisor in helping to create a triangular space, offering a third perspective to counteract the potentially regressive and enmeshed dyadic relationship of therapy (see, e.g., Solomon, 2007). Supervisor and supervisee necessarily have different viewpoints. The supervisor can take an overall perspective in that they are at one remove from the heat of the therapeutic situation, they are likely to have more experience of therapeutic work and more general understanding of psychodynamics, but the supervisee is the one with the immediate experience and everyday knowledge of the patient and the emotions generated by the interaction.

For both parties to communicate and develop an understanding of what is going on with the patient, in terms of unconscious dynamics, it is important that there is a basic level of trust on both sides, trust in terms of good intentions, a commitment to the process, and a desire to create an atmosphere of tolerance and openness, a space to think as many writers have described it (see, e.g., Mollon, 1997).

We need to create an environment where learning can take place; this cannot be taken for granted. The task is difficult partly because we can be lulled into a false sense of security. When supervision is going well, it is rewarding and interesting and there is a sense of a partnership, in terms of two people working together to try to understand something about the patient's emotional life. We can let our guard down a little, play with the material, speculate and free associate. When we are suddenly jolted into a different sort of reality, when a problem or impasse develops, it can take us by surprise. Sometimes this is because without realizing it a good working relationship has moved into something more collusive or complacent, which needs to be challenged.

This book considers the supervisory relationship and ways in which this can be facilitated or undermined by factors that may not be immediately obvious to supervisors at the beginning of their careers. Experienced supervisors also need to keep them in mind, as this is not simply a matter of conscious intention. We all bring our own difficulties, tendencies and habitual ways of relating to the task of supervision, not all of which will be known to us at any particular moment. Some writing on supervision seems to start from the point of view that the supervisor, aided by their own therapy, has been able to eliminate such difficulties, in contrast to the patient under discussion and the supervisee. But since we are all influenced by our unconscious, we have to take responsibility for monitoring our state of mind and thinking about our own continuing learning as supervisors, just as we do for learning from our work as therapists.

Difficulties may arise from idiosyncratic factors – people are very different, and a particular combination of supervisor/supervisee may give rise to frustration, deep conflict or impasse. We bring different expectations to supervision too, based on our own experiences and our individual differences. So we cannot ignore the individual qualities that we bring to the process as supervisors and supervisees. Nevertheless, I think that it is the complexities inherent in the process and in the situations being thought about which account for many of the difficulties. Some of these are considered briefly below.

The complexity of aims and purposes of supervision requires us to think about the boundaries of the task. Supervision has an educational function but is not the same as more formal teaching or tutorial support. We need to assess and monitor progress but when the monitoring function becomes predominant, it is a matter for concern, often implying a lack of trust in the supervisee. Supervision is not therapy, though we may need to acknowledge difficulties and take on a more supportive role at times. How do we begin to think about where to draw the line? As the following example suggests, sometimes there is a discrepancy – in this case quite an extreme polarisation – between the views of the supervisor and the supervisee.

Tony, a supervisor in private practice, was approached by Angela, who was looking for a supervisor for her work in a counselling service. She explained that the requirement was for supervision once a month – that was all that was needed. Tony went along with this to begin with but as they began to work together felt increasingly uneasy; sessions tended to be used to present piecemeal fragments of sessions and queries about practice, relating to a number of clients, far more than could be realistically thought about in the time. He was finding it hard to get any sense of Angela's work, in terms of how she was with clients or how his supervision was helping her to develop as a practitioner. He thought about this and suggested they meet more often.

In the ensuing discussion it became clear that they had very different ideas about supervision. Angela initially seemed to feel quite insulted and infantilised at the suggestion of more supervisory hours; she thought it was a criticism of her practice and her readiness to work as a counsellor. When she expanded on her ideas she realised that she thought of supervision, once a person was qualified, as primarily a way of safeguarding the client, a monitoring function, rather than an opportunity for her to learn more. She wanted to know, in rather simplistic terms, what she should do in specific instances. She was open to being told what to do but did not see the need to think further about the detail or what might lie behind the suggestion. Tony however was much more concerned with helping her develop as a counsellor and saw supervision as primarily educational and supportive. At this early stage in their relationship, he didn't feel he could help in this way if they met only once a month. However, he had also found her approach disconcerting, particularly in relation to his comments and criticism – maybe he did need to be more curious about details of her practice.

Complexity of aims and purposes of supervision

The above example obviously raises a number of questions which are not only about the function of supervision. We might wonder about the way in which the supervisory contract was set up, and the level of experience and understanding of both of the participants for example. But there is inevitably a tension between the two aims of helping the supervisee develop as a therapist (the educational function) and safeguarding the interests of the patient (more of a monitoring function), which many writers have considered. Both of these functions can create anxiety in the supervisee; if the monitoring side of it predominates, they may worry that their practice might be found to be ineffective or even harmful. But developing and learning more as a therapist also brings its own anxieties, as we shall see in Chapter 3.

From a historical point of view, the educational function of supervision developed first, particularly in relation to analytic training (see below, and Chapter 4, on the relationship of supervision practice to developments in analytic theory), but the proliferation of psychotherapy and counselling courses in the last 30 years, and the pressures to regulate these, has also led to the monitoring function becoming more prominent. The British Association Counselling and Psychotherapy recognises this in the requirements for practising counsellors, including experienced practitioners, to receive a specified amount of supervision, on a monthly basis, throughout their working life. This has not always been true of some branches of the psychotherapy profession, where there has been a prevailing attitude that once qualified, a practitioner would not need supervision – indeed, getting a qualification implied a capacity to work independently which might be stifled if supervision continued. This seems to be changing; the introduction of continuing professional development requirements in organisations such as the British Psychoanalytic Council seems to have led to a reassessment of the importance of supervision for experienced practitioners. Hester Solomon (op. cit.) in a recent paper argues strongly for continuing supervision after qualification, seeing this as the expression of a mature and ethical professional attitude.

In practice, as Richard Jones (1989) points out, the two aims, of safeguarding the well-being of the patient as well as assisting the development of the supervisee, normally fit together well, since a therapist who has been able to build on their own learning and development is much more likely to work well with the patient. We might all agree that we aim first of all to help the supervisee to understand the patient and work more effectively to help them in their own understanding of their difficulties. Of course, being a trainee puts very specific pressures on both supervisor and supervisee which complicate the relationship, which we will consider in Chapter 3.

But Jones also draws attention to the possibility that these aims can be in conflict – and in practice different writers on the subject value these functions to a different extent. He quotes Robert Langs (1979) who is clear that the supervisor's first responsibility is to the patient. 'Any time a supervisor has an influence on a treatment situation, the patient and his needs must come first . . . . I am stressing only that the supervisor must have as his first concern that the patient receive the therapy he needs' (p. 18).

In extreme situations, where a patient's life is in danger, the supervisor has to use their authority to safeguard the situation. But often the situation is less clear-cut; it may take time to develop a view as to what is in the best interests of the patient. In addition the supervisor can only work through the supervisee; no matter how 'correct' we may think ourselves to be, we are not the patient's therapist. A very common situation in supervision is that where the supervisor urges the supervisee to take up a particular aspect of the patient's thinking or behaviour in the session, and a level of frustration sets in on the supervisor's part when the supervisee is not able to do this, perhaps because they have a somewhat idealised view of the patient and the issues they bring to therapy. The supervisee in this situation can feel chastened and somewhat demoralised. Jones writes of the adverse implications of continuing to push the supervisee, and points out that as supervisors we have to be continually on our guard against nurturing any narcissistic tendencies to think that we always know best, at the expense of the supervisee's learning and their relationship with the patient or client. Sometimes it is a matter of experience; it can be very difficult, for example, for a counsellor beginning to see clients to understand how important they might be, at an unconscious level, to the client. This can result in the significance of absences and breaks not being fully appreciated; it might take some while to integrate theory and practice, as the following example shows:

> Miriam, a counsellor working in a university brought Cassie, a student she was seeing long term, to supervision. The summer break was approaching and the supervisor, thinking of Cassie's history of losses and abandonments, emphasised to her supervisee the need to address the subject of the break. She was mindful of the fact that over three months would elapse before she could be seen again, since Cassie had to return home as soon as her exams were over to look after her younger siblings. The supervisor had a sense that Miriam wasn't in touch with the depth of feeling that this situation (the lost sessions) might engender. She made this point, but she had a sense of it not sinking in.
>
> However, the psychic reality of the situation was soon brought home very forcibly to Miriam. She was sitting in her office in the last week of term, when Cassie appeared, half an hour before what would have been her last session before the holidays, had she been able to stay for it. She

*had taken her brother's car and driven a hundred miles to get to the
university. She didn't think she would be able to see Miriam – she just
wanted to check that she was there. (In the event, Miriam, horrified at
the apparent risks Cassie had taken – she said she had driven well over
the speed limit – was able to offer her some time.)*

Clearly this is a complex situation requiring a certain amount of
unravelling – but Miriam certainly learned, in a very vivid way,
something about the strength of her client's attachments. The experience made her able to think about similar situations and interpret
breaks and absences in a much more cogent way, that made sense to
her clients.

In this case, as will often happen, the supervisor was able to be
patient with the supervisee and allow her to learn from experience.
But the needs of the client or patient have to be thought about. Sometimes, focussing on the supervisee and their learning, rather than
thinking about the impact on the patient, can result, as Jones suggests, in a collusive relationship developing with the supervisee,
where there is implicit agreement that certain issues will not be challenged in supervision or in the related counselling or therapy. As he
writes, giving priority to either patient or supervisee results in the
'drawback . . . that they entail a departure for the analytic attitude on
the supervisor's part'.

This then is the central difficulty in supervision; how do we maintain an overview and a sense of balance – or an awareness – of all
the factors which are working against this, not only in the reported
interaction between the supervisee and the patient, but also in supervision and in the wider context of the work? We also have to be
aware of our own characteristic tendencies, perhaps in the direction
of avoiding conflict or alternatively, of pushing our own point of
view. These questions relate to the question of the way in which we
take up the authority which goes with being a supervisor, an issue
which will be further discussed in Chapter 3.

The complexity of the aims cited above can result in tension in
terms of the supervisor's role. Many of the readers of this book will
also be involved in education, therapy and management of counsellors and therapists in other contexts, as well as supervision; when
under pressure, it is easy to fall back on more familiar ways of relating. New counsellors and therapists often have to abandon other
modes of working in helping relationships (see Chapter 2) and learn
not to ask too many questions or give advice. In the same way, supervisors also have to think about and clarify what is required from

them as a supervisor. Below we consider briefly some further aspects of the different functions of supervision.

The educational aspect of supervision

As has already been stated, supervisors traditionally have an educative role. One of the main aims when working with supervisees at the beginning of their careers is to allow the supervisee to develop a lively sense of the elements of the psychodynamic approach by seeing how concepts relate to practice. This can be achieved in various ways, from a didactic approach involving specific suggestions to a more facilitative approach, where the supervisee is encouraged to come to their own conclusions. Both of these approaches have their place in supervision; when supervisees begin therapeutic work, they can find it very containing to have some concrete suggestions for interventions. But if this process goes on too long, or predominates in place of thinking together about the patient, then it can become irksome and constrictive. This draws attention to the need to think about the needs of the individual supervisee, in terms of the stage they have reached in the process of becoming a practitioner. We may also have to consider how we can help our individual supervisees to learn; some seem to be relatively prepared to take in what is being said, others have to learn by experience or by experimentation. As the above example of Miriam and Cassie shows, we all need the experience of working with clients or patients to bring alive and deepen our understanding of the theory. Ultimately we have to help the supervisee to find their own voice; as Mary Twyman (2007) writes, we need to value the qualities and previous experience of the supervisee and help them to develop to their full potential in their therapeutic work, not to impose a particular style upon the supervisee.

Jean Arundale (2007), considering the question of the qualities and experience that supervisors need, concludes that psychodynamic supervision involves above all the transmission of internalised psychoanalytic values; it is not a matter of techniques or skills but of establishing a relationship where beliefs and goals can be shared, having the quality of an apprenticeship for the supervisee. This implies a degree of maturity in the supervisor as a psychotherapist, and this seems crucial to taking up the supervisory role. By maturity I am not implying that a supervisor has the answers, rather the reverse, that they are able to tolerate ambiguities and uncertainties while being prepared to think about the patient and generate useful hypotheses on their situation.

Monitoring and managing

The monitoring function of supervision (in terms of their interaction with the client or patient) is one that often causes anxiety to new supervisors, particularly when they are supervising trainees or others where they have clinical responsibility for the well-being of the patient. There are additional difficulties if the supervisor has no input into the nature of patients that are allocated to inexperienced trainees. In this circumstance the supervisor may find they have responsibility for maintaining standards and safeguarding the interest of the patient but have no power to manage the situation at the beginning of the process. Many writers (e.g., Langs, op. cit.) advocate a separation of management and supervisory functions, arguing that the supervisor needs to safeguard a space where the supervisee can be free to be honest about their thoughts and feelings about the patient and their interventions without being overlooked on a day-to-day basis by a training organisation. But in practice, management and supervisory functions are often combined, and sometimes it has its advantages. When supervising placement counsellors, for example, being able to carry out assessments also means that the supervisor has some knowledge of the client and their issues, with which to compare the account from the supervisee.

Supervision versus therapy: supporting the supervisee

As we shall see in Chapter 4, supervision in the psychoanalytic tradition was originally seen as something that belonged in the student's own analysis. This was rooted in the assumption that the patient's difficulties could be considered independently of the psychoanalyst's experience in the session; any feelings that disturbed the analyst's ability to take up a neutral stance needed consideration in the training analysis. Since we now recognise the importance of thinking about our own countertransference as a guide to the patient's relationship with their internal objects, emotions experienced during sessions become highly relevant to our thinking about the patient. Currently, psychotherapists and most counsellors training in the psychodynamic tradition are expected to have their own therapy while training, which makes it easier to draw a bound-ary between supervision and therapy. It also allows them to give some consideration to the origin of these feelings. But the question of where and how to draw the line continues to concern supervi-sors, particularly in circumstances where the supervisees are health professionals who have no experience of personal therapy.

There are a number of aspects of this dilemma. Supervisors may find themselves pressured at times to take up a more therapeu-tic stance, in the sense that they may find themselves commenting where they think that a particular characteristic of the supervisee is getting in the way of the work. When I am supervising I feel free, potentially, to make such an observation, but I try not to get drawn into detailed further discussion, particularly if the person concerned is in therapy.

In addition, supervisees will often let supervisors know of diffi-culties or crises in their personal life and I think that it is important to listen, and part of the supportive function of supervision, in the service of understanding the overall context in which the supervisee is working. I am prepared for the fact that some supervisees want to tell me that an aspect of their work has brought up a particular issue, and I will acknowledge its importance. On the whole I have found that supervisees are relatively bounded in their personal revelations; normally, they tell us as a point of information, not to challenge the boundaries. A common example is the situation where a member of the supervisee's family is causing anxiety, in a way which may echo situations with clients. Under these circumstances supervisees may feel they need the supervisor to keep in mind the kind of pressure they are under, and help them not to over identify with the client.

Supporting the supervisee is also an important aspect of helping them deal with the ever present anxiety of working therapeutically with people who present with difficult, complex issues; if the super-visor can listen to and tolerate their anxieties in supervision, they are more likely to be able to manage their anxieties in the session. In this respect, as so often, the supervisor can find themselves mod-elling a containing stance. I also find that all supervisees, particularly those working in institutions and having some management respon-sibility, sometimes arrive at sessions needing to begin by simply articulating their preoccupations and concerns – there is a cathartic value to supervision.

This brings me to a further thought on supervision, which is that sometimes when there are no patients to think about it can be useful – and ultimately helpful – to allow for time to talk about matters which are not directly related to clinical work; very often a theme develops which has a bearing on our understanding of the work. Thomas Ogden (2005), writing about supervision, considers this matter; under the heading 'On the importance of having time to waste' he writes of the necessity of valuing a state of reverie where ideas are allowed to float to the surface, and points out that in some circumstances, sticking rigidly to clinical material can have a defensive quality. It is a salutary reminder that being able to play with ideas and free associate is also an important part of supervision.

Some definitions and an outline of the contents of the book

The book looks at supervision from a psychodynamic perspective and this term needs further definition; in this context, I use 'psychodynamic' to refer to ideas that developed originally from psychoanalytic ideas. Any definition is bound to raise questions as well as answer them but I can only write from my own experience and the ideas that have informed my own practice as a counsellor, psychotherapist and a supervisor are those of Freud, Klein and Winnicott and others working in the same tradition. This implies, at its simplest, that I am assuming a dynamic relationship between our conscious and unconscious worlds, with all that this implies in terms of conflict, anxieties and defences. These dynamics can best be explored in a bounded, consistent setting where attention is paid to the effects of breaks and discontinuities. Also implied is the idea that past experiences will influence current relationships, including that with the therapist. Transference and countertransference are concepts which are central to my understanding of counselling, therapy and supervision. I am assuming that most of the readers of this book will be therapists working in this tradition; however, those wanting an account of psychodynamic ideas as they relate to counselling will find this in Laurence Spurling's book (2004) *An Introduction to Psychodynamic Counselling* in the same series as this book.

Readers will of course have their own favourite theories, and the world of psychoanalytic psychotherapy and psychodynamic counselling is beset with disagreements and at the very least differences in emphases. For example, practitioners within different traditions place a different emphasis on the inner world versus the external circumstances of the patient, and have different explanations for the difficulties the session reveals – and the way we conceptualise this will affect the interpretations we might consider in supervision. We may place a different emphasis on building an alliance with the patient as opposed to challenging them, and this may also affect what we think about the timing of interpretations. And, like our supervisees, we may have largely implicit, possibly unexamined theories about the way in which we conceptualise the work, which need to be thought about; this is a task for our own continuing professional development.

Throughout the book I have used case illustrations, sometimes small vignettes, sometimes more extended examples, to illustrate the points I am making. They have been chosen to represent common situations in supervision. In certain cases I have asked for permission from supervisees to write an account of a disguised situation, and have shown them the account. All of those consulted agreed, very generously, that I could include the material, sometime subject to small amendments. Other examples are composites, chosen to make a point about circumstances that can arise in supervision; they are based on my experience but there has been an element of creativity in putting together ideas, characters and circumstances. I have tried to convey the essence of the experience in a vivid way. Readers will probably have in mind their own versions of the aggressive supervisee who challenges their authority, and the supervisee who finds it difficult not to ask the client too many questions. But we also know that sometimes supervisors can unwittingly make things worse. I have tried to start from the assumption that supervisors are human and that being able to reflect on situations and practice can enable us to be a more helpful version of ourselves as supervisors. In writing the examples I have of course been able to draw on my experience as a counsellor, psychotherapist and supervisee over many years, as well as a supervisor, trying to remember and profit from earlier experiences. And in common with most of the people reading this book there is also at a deeper level the experience of having been a patient.

I use the terms 'counsellor', 'psychotherapist', and 'therapist' in relation to the supervisee being considered, and those they are working with as 'clients' and 'patients'. While these terms are by no means interchangeable, their use in a particular situation sometimes indicates context; psychotherapists working in institutions may be given the title 'counsellor', or vice versa, and those they are working with are also called 'clients' or 'patients'. However, the nomenclature may be significant in terms of the role of the institution but it does not necessarily indicate anything in terms of the sophistication or experience of the practitioner who is bringing work to supervision. And an analytic attitude can be used to inform work in any context.

As we have seen, supervision is a complex matter. In subsequent chapters we will consider aspects of the tasks of supervision in more detail, as follows.

Chapter 2, 'Beginning supervision', is intended for those who are supervising for the first time, and considers in particular the needs of relatively inexperienced counsellors or therapists. In this context we think about the importance of providing a bounded setting for supervision, partly as a way of modelling an attention to boundary issues for supervisees but also, crucially, as a way of containing our supervisees' anxieties about beginning therapeutic work. We also consider in a very rudimentary way the practical tasks of supervision, and what we might expect from supervisees.

Chapter 3, 'The emotional experience of learning and teaching in supervision', considers further the sources of anxiety in supervision; we think about what is implied in learning in this context, including the experiential nature of the process, difficulties in managing uncertainty, the contribution of different expectations and assumptions and the often unconscious anxieties relating to authority, particularly in the context of training and assessment. We consider how the attitude of the supervisor and the dynamics of the training institution can affect the level of anxiety in supervisees.

In Chapter 4 we explore the function of psychodynamic theory in supervision; it will be seen that developments of theory relating to supervision have been related closely to the development of psychoanalytic theory; in particular, the development of the concept of internal objects paved the way for a different view to be taken of relationships in therapy and the manifestations of transference and countertransference, leading to new ideas about the part these phenomena play in supervision. We also consider a model of the needs of supervisees at different stages of development, and ways in which theory can help us in supervision.

In Chapter 5 we return to a consideration of the process of supervision, and elaborate on aspects of the task of understanding the supervisee's work with the client or patient. We consider the role of the process recording in beginning to understand what has gone on in the session and the way in which this can lead to thinking in more depth about the nature of the countertransference. We think about ways of understanding and working with the inevitable enactments in the therapeutic situation. The importance of being aware of the roles we take up in relation to the supervisee and their material is stressed, since this may be a reflection of the dynamics of the session with the patient.

The next three chapters deal with aspects of the context of supervision and the work being supervised. Chapter 6 looks at the particular advantages and complications of group supervision; this is likely to be the first experience of supervision for many supervisees and is often the first opportunity many of us have to take up the role of supervisor. We can see that group dynamics create their own difficulties, which I think about in terms of Bion's framework of basic assumption groups. But groups can also demonstrate a type of parallel process, which we have thought about in Chapter 4, where the functioning of the group can provide a clue to otherwise unnoticed aspects of the relationship between the client and the supervisee.

In Chapter 7 the subject of institutional dynamics and the supervision of those working in organisations is considered. Counsellors and therapists working in institutions are subject to additional pressures relating to the way in which the institution manages anxiety. I outline some theories that will be useful in this context, those based on psychoanalytic theory, group relations theory and systems theory and how these can inform supervision practice. Working in an institution may involve thinking differently about the transference, for example, and there is likely to be increased pressure on the therapist to take action rather than reflect.

Chapter 8, 'Working with difference', explores in particular the issues that might be involved in supervising work where the participants are of a different colour or ethnic group. The necessity of thinking about and addressing this issue is discussed, although it inevitably brings up very difficult feelings, whatever our own ethnic background. The implications of not doing so, however, might be to entrench existing disadvantages for members of minority groups. The chapter also considers the impact of gender and sexuality, age and disability on therapy and supervision.

In Chapter 9, 'Challenges and dilemmas in supervision', I explore in particular the difficulties of supervising therapists who are working with suicidal or seriously ill patients. This situation calls on all the resources of the supervisor, in helping the therapist to contain their anxiety, and it may also involve a more focussed approach in terms of thinking with the supervisee about appropriate interventions. Other situations, including difficulties within the supervisory relationship, are considered briefly. What all these situations have in common is that they challenge the supervisor's ways of working and thinking, making it difficult to keep a reflective stance.

The book concludes with an appendix of addresses of organisations that the reader may find useful.

Summary and conclusions

In this introductory chapter I have outlined some of the factors that make supervision difficult at times. I see these as relating primarily to the different functions that supervision is expected to fulfil. Supervision is not the same as teaching, management, supporting or therapy but yet there are elements of these processes in supervision. Supervisor and supervisee may have different views of where the boundary should be drawn. The chapter goes on to outline the contents of the book and provide some details of definitions.

The following points emerge from the discussion in this chapter:

- The tasks of supervision are complex and require the supervisor to keep in mind the balance between the needs of the supervisee, in terms of their education and development, and those of the client or patient they are working with.
- This implies that supervisors need to have got to the point in their own development when they have a degree of maturity as practitioners, with an integrated understanding of theory and practice, so that they can put their own anxieties aside and focus on the supervisee and their patient.
- Different supervisors will place different emphases on the balance between educative, and monitoring and other functions. These may relate to their own experience and that of the supervisee and also to the context in which they are working.
- While supervision needs to steer clear of moving towards a therapeutic function, there will be times when supervisees need to experience our support to allow them to focus on the patient.

2

BEGINNING SUPERVISION

Introduction

This chapter outlines some of the main considerations when beginning supervision; it is intended both for new supervisors and for
supervisors working with new or inexperienced counsellors and
therapists. Even within this category of supervisees there is a great
deal of variation, for example, in terms of psychodynamic understanding and whether this understanding is explicitly shared. At
one extreme might be candidates undergoing a psychoanalytic psychotherapy training, seeing patients several times a week, where
there is a relatively sophisticated understanding of concepts in theory but there is a need for these to be developed and grounded in
practice so that the supervisee can eventually function safely as an
independent practitioner. Those supervising such trainees will usually be very experienced practitioners. Much of this chapter however
focuses on the supervision of those at a much earlier point in their
development as therapists.

New supervisees and some of their anxieties

Working with a patient or client in a new context arouses anxiety,
however experienced and knowledgeable we might be. Bion (1979)
described any meeting between individuals as an 'emotional storm'
and I think this gets close to describing the kind of anxiety that
can be generated in trainee psychotherapists by taking on a training
patient. Consciously there is the ever present worry that the patient
may leave, and the training will be compromised. Anxiety also stems
from the unfamiliarity of the intensity of the contact in a therapeutic setting as well as the nature of the difficulties presented. And, as
with all training situations, there is the additional anxiety of being
assessed in supervision. We consider this situation in more depth in
Chapter 3.

However, the most likely situation for those beginning to practice as supervisors is that of supervising people working at a less intensive level, as counsellors in various contexts. They too will be anxious about their first experiences with clients. Their numbers are increasing; the proliferation of counselling courses, many of which require their trainees to find a voluntary placement, together with the British Association for Counselling and Psychotherapy's requirements in terms of supervised practice, contributes to the demand for supervision. Again, there may well be a shared framework of psychodynamic ideas but the supervisees are likely to have very little experience of what these mean in practice. One of the tasks of supervision is to help the trainee to elaborate their understanding of concepts and how these relate to their clients and the relationship.

In addition, voluntary agencies and any organisation working with people in distress have become aware of the need to consider issues and obligations relating to their Duty of Care. This means there is a need to develop high standards of supervision of voluntary counsellors. A further influence on demand for supervision is the interest of professionals working in related fields to obtain psychodynamic supervision or consultation to help contain anxieties connected with difficult dynamics in the workplace.

It is likely therefore that one's first experience of supervising will involve thinking about the needs of counsellors at the very beginning of their professional life. They may be students who have completed a couple of terms or a year of a course or they could be volunteers who have completed some sessions on listening skills and have not formally studied psychodynamic theory. Despite their inexperience, and the best intentions of their managers and others in their work settings or agencies, they may find themselves working with very challenging, disturbed or traumatised clients. For example, bereavement counselling is commonly set up on a voluntary basis, perhaps on the basis that bereavement is not an illness, but something of which we will all have experience. Yet volunteers may find themselves very challenged as the following example shows:

Ellie had worked effectively with her first client, a woman in her middle years who was coming to terms with the death of an apparently very domineering father. Her second client, Miss C, approached the service shortly after her sister's death by suicide, having found her sister's body lying in the bathroom of her flat. Ellie agreed to take on this client, who as usual was visited in her own home. It soon became clear that visiting Miss C was going to be a very different experience for Ellie. Miss C was understandably very angry, upset and traumatised and needed to go over and over the details of the discovery of the body, crying angrily and persistently, and asking what good would this counselling do? It couldn't take away this awful feeling, and the images that kept intruding into her mind. Ellie felt anxious, deskilled and overwhelmed. She knew that she would probably have to go through this experience many times; how could Miss C face her feelings of anger, horror and disgust if Ellie could not survive a second-hand account of the event?

This example raises a number of issues and is put in as a reminder of the sense of shock and anxiety that working with our first few clients might provoke. Readers can probably recall their own early experiences. It is not only to do with the nature of the issues with which clients may present, but also to do with a function of the concerns that trainees or volunteers bring to their work. To begin with, we tend to idealise the work, our clients or patients and the version of ourselves that is there in the room with the client. We have an idea of being useful and helpful, and of course none of us would do this work if we did not have a belief in its ultimate value. Our first experiences show us that it is more complicated than that. In the above example, Ellie was dismayed at how difficult she found it to just be with the client, in contrast to her work with the first client where she had been able to identify with the issues presented and to be empathetic.

Trainee counsellors are not yet confident of their ability to contain the client's anxieties, partly because they may not have had the opportunity to develop their own sense of containment. In addition to being at the beginning of their counselling career, they may also be relatively new to their own personal therapy – if in fact they are in therapy, which is not the case for many voluntary counsellors, or professionals from other areas. Since they may lack a sense of their own boundaries, they are particularly likely to be affected by disturbance, chaos and madness in the client. This seemed to be at the heart of Ellie's experience when it was talked about – she wondered if she could manage to survive psychically the sheer volume of distress and disturbing images.

A different concern is about the challenge of having to work in what may be a quite unfamiliar way. People who have had experience of working therapeutically in other contexts may find that they need to set aside their usual ways of working. In many professions in the health service, for example, asking the patient questions is an important part of trying to identify problems and think about a diagnosis. Thinking psychodynamically, we know that although this approach may comfort some patients in the short run, it is not ultimately helpful for various reasons; the patient needs to feel free to bring whatever is on their mind and also needs to accept responsibility for what is brought to, and discussed in, a session. Others, who have been used to taking a more didactic role or one where advice or actual practical help was part of the job, will have to struggle with their urges to be active in this way in a counselling session. The temptation to retreat to familiar patterns of working has complex origins, some within the supervisee and some resulting from pressures from the patient and will be considered later in the chapter.

The need to create a bounded setting for supervision

Supervision is not the same as therapy as we have already discussed (Chapter 1). But because of the above-mentioned anxieties of counsellors at the beginning of their careers, there is a particular need for a setting which provides consistency and a space where the experience of working with patients can be thought about and concerns explored. Providing this setting is really the first task of supervision. Many writers thinking about this subject pay tribute to Winnicott's idea (1962) that the mother needs outside support if she is to respond sensitively and appropriately to the baby's needs; he comments that 'usually the husband shields her from external reality and so enables her to protect her child from unpredictable external phenomena to which the child must react' (p. 71). Casement (1985, p. 35) considers the situation of the inexperienced therapist, and writes:

> ... the supervisor has a crucially important function in holding the student during this opening phase of clinical work-while he or she is learning to hold the patient analytically. The supervisor provides a form of control, making it safe for the therapist and patient to become analytically engaged, and helping the student to understand and to contain what is being presented by the patient.

What is implied in this holding and control? It suggests a need for supervisors to provide something of the same sort of bounded experience as they would for their own patients. Central to this way of thinking is the idea of the setting, or therapeutic frame, a phrase first used by Marion Milner (1952) and taken up by many writers since that time. One of the most accessible accounts is that of Anne Gray

(1994) who writes of the concept and the way in which the frame allows the therapist to allow the expression of hitherto repressed emotions and to contain them symbolically for the client. Going on to think about supervision she draws a parallel between the containment and understanding provided for the client and the supervisory function (p. 118).

The American analyst, Robert Langs (1994), who has written very extensively on supervision in the context of analytical training, suggests very specific rules for the conduct of supervision, and also points out some of the implications that result from breaking the frame, no matter how necessary this may seem because of practical considerations. His stance is that very often the patient's material is a commentary on the therapist's handling of the therapeutic frame and that likewise a supervisee will respond to a supervisor's breaking the frame with various indications – in the material presented or other behaviour – that they do not feel securely held. Langs makes the point that even if deviations from a secured frame are justifiable by external circumstances, there will always be unconscious reactions to them. He also writes of the conflicting desires that we all have (p. 70); a person 'deeply needs and wishes a secure frame' but this will at the same time create anxieties, which we will attempt to alleviate by various forms of acting out. He writes (p. 70):

> In supervision then, all parties, as human beings, inevitably will find themselves mired in, or creating for themselves – deliberately or inadvertently – all manner of frame alterations. Securing frames requires understanding, strong motivation and effort – they are not a consequence of our natural inclinations.

The following example illustrates a consequence of breaking the supervisory frame, as well being as a reminder that what you do is more important than what you say:

> *I needed to cancel a weekly group supervision of counsellors working in a community counselling service. Since the two supervisees involved were beginners and had fairly new clients, I offered to talk to them both individually over the telephone in the course of the following few days. This seemed to work well, but two weeks later when one of them was reporting on a missed session, he told me that he has been surprised that the client hadn't turned up as he had altered the time of the session at the client's request. Surprised, I asked what had made him do this (it ran counter to his training and the discussions we had*

*previously had about the setting) and he answered in rather confused
and vague terms, of 'wanting to be helpful to the client, as she had
another appointment', and so on. It was only later that I realised that
I had probably contributed to this confusion in the mind of the supervisee by offering an alternative for his own cancelled session. Both of
us were trying over hard to 'be helpful', and my offer of help outside the normal frame had apparently been counterproductive in this
situation.*

Sometimes it seems that there is no alternative to rearranging or
in some way altering the frame of supervision – as occasionally
in therapy – but this was a reminder to me that it is important to
monitor the situation and check for unexpected effects.

Langs goes on to write that given the inevitability, at times, of
aspects of the setting being altered, recognising and re-securing the
frame is a mark of a good supervisor and supervisee. His recommendations for setting up a contract for supervision are set out
below:

- the place, time, length of session and frequency of sessions should
  be fixed for the duration of the supervision.
- he outlines arrangements for the paying of fees, comparable for
  that for psychotherapy.
- total privacy, implying a one-to-one relationship.
- confidentiality, implying that the process is free from the need to
  expose the trainee for assessment purposes.

(Langs 1994, pp. 72–110)

Many supervisors would agree that these conditions provide a baseline for setting up a supervision arrangement, although they may be
difficult to adhere to in practice.

For example, his recommendation of individual supervision once
a week, although the norm in many circumstances, particularly
during training as a psychotherapist, is not always possible for counsellors in training; the financial resources may not be there. And
there are also positive advantages of group supervision as Chapter 6
will show. The role of supervision as a way of teaching and consol-
idating learning means that supervisors are often required to write
reports on their supervisees, and it is difficult to think of a way round
this – assessment is necessary and the inherent tension between feeling free to be honest and the desire to present one's work in its
best aspects has to be faced. Privacy and confidentiality may be

affected by agency rules about disclosure of information. And the question of fees may not be a relevant consideration for many supervisees who get supervision as part of the contract for working in an agency.

Freud (1913) wrote of his rules for the practice of psychoanalytic treatment as 'recommendations' which might not be unequivocally followed, since there were many variations in the circumstances (psychic or otherwise) of treatment. He pointed out however that 'these circumstances do not prevent us from laying down a procedure for the physician which is effective on average' (p. 123). In the same way, supervisors need to provide a setting which is generally robust enough to allow counsellors to bear the vicissitudes of the encounter with the client and then reveal honestly what went on in the session.

A further function of a bounded setting for working as a counsellor becomes apparent to supervisees once work with clients begins, in that its regularity and consistency become an important baseline against which variations in all sort of differences can be measured and demonstrated in supervision. These might be in the behaviour of the client within a session or in different sessions, differences between clients and variations in the way the counsellor habitually or occasionally reacts. In other words, the session functions as a set situation in the sense that Winnicott (1941) means when he describes the reactions of different babies to an offer of play within a consistent clinical setting. The fact that his procedure with the children is the same every time means that the nuances of the baby's behaviour can throw light on their way of relating to the world. Quoting this example, Spurling (2004) highlights the importance of a regular structure and context for working with clients, in terms of developing a consistent way of viewing the special characteristics of the client, and there are similar advantages to this degree of consistency, in supervision.

The bounded nature of the counselling setting is particularly important for people seeing their very first clients; one frequently asked question is 'how do I know what are my feelings and what belongs to the client?' It is sometime hard for supervisees to accept that there is no easy answer to this question, that it is something that all practitioners have to think about throughout their working life. It is a matter of careful observation of the setting and what happens within it, including one's own reactions. Often, getting a second client throws light on the respective contributions of the first client and the counsellor, and this can be a great relief for someone stuck in a difficult transference/countertransference situation, as the following example shows:

Linda was seeing her first client, Miss W, a voluble young woman undergoing a personal and family crisis. The client made it clear that she liked Linda and often tried to draw her into a more personal relationship, admiring her clothes, asking about her weekend and generally trying to introduce a social aspect to the counselling. Linda resisted this, but found it hard to intervene in the sessions, and very often found that the only way she could do so was by asking questions. This pattern proved very hard to change. Linda knew she shouldn't do this but, when challenged, thought that perhaps that was what she was used to, having been a market researcher, and that old habits were hard to break. For some months there was a very painful 'stuck' feeling to the supervision whenever Miss W was discussed, with the supervisor exhorting Linda to think about her interventions and feeling, and being, rather over critical and Linda feeling pinioned by both the supervisor and the client.

The supervisor realised that this questioning was a very common tendency in new counsellors but found herself wondering whether there was anything special that was contributing to this, speculating that it was Linda's overall anxiety about beginning work as a counsellor that was being activated, although they both agreed that the client was very intrusive and that perhaps the questions served a defensive function, of keeping Miss W at bay.

Once Linda started work with the second client it could be seen much more clearly that the questions had something to do with the dynamics of working with Miss W, since the situation in this latter case was very different, with Linda being much more reflective in the sessions with the new client. This realisation allowed a much freer exploration of the complexities of Linda's relationship with Miss W and the nature of the identifications going on. The questions appeared to be related not only to the blurring of boundaries which were a feature of Miss W's attempts to get closer to Linda but also to something that came up when Linda managed to explore the curiosity that Miss W showed towards her; Miss W had many unsatisfied questions about her own past (she had been adopted as a baby and knew nothing about her biological parents). Miss W began to allow Linda some space in the session; once she felt less immobilised, the work took on a different emphasis.

The supervisor noted that it felt much more possible to cooperate on thinking together about the client once this situation had become unstuck.

The tasks of supervision

We have already seen that supervision needs to provide a model of the setting which supervisees need to create for their clients, a subject which also needs to be thought about in detail, depending on their level of expertise, before they begin work. This is a way of developing an understanding of the concept of boundaries in the context of work with clients.

Supervisors know from experience that attention to the details of the setting is important. New supervisees may be inclined to dismiss these as trivial if they are waiting impatiently to begin work. But supervisees vary: many are quite anxious about these matters at the beginning, and find it a great relief to know that they can be thought about in supervision. Some know from experience that these matters are important to them in their own therapy. Others find it irksome; sometimes this attitude if not challenged results in a number of thoughtless attacks on the boundaries (for example, not thinking it important that the sessions start and finish on time). Such matters as the wording of letters giving the time of the first session, when to introduce the subject of the contract, how to talk about missed sessions, holidays and the collection of fees (if this is part of the deal) are all important.

The way in which we present ourselves to a client is also something that needs to be discussed. The question of the degree of self-disclosure on the part of the counsellor often comes up. Supervisees often say, 'But what if I get asked?' (for some personal piece of information) almost as though they feel obliged to answer any question that is put to them. But when we begin this work, we may not have any confidence in our own ability to work psychodynamically – we may think that withholding information is churlish and will drive the client away. One concern that seems to come up with virtually every trainee is the question of how to deal with questions about the counsellor's training and experience. Many agencies now have a policy on this subject which makes explicit the approach that trainees should adopt, but if that is not the case, it is important to give the supervisee time to think about the balance that is needed between giving factual information and exploring the client's anxieties about the quality of treatment they are getting.

The first sessions

Once work with clients has started, supervisions need to focus on a number of interrelated basic tasks. This is very much an outline; they will be elaborated on elsewhere in the book, and of course the way in which they are carried out depends on the stage that the supervisee has reached. They include:

- getting an account of what has transpired between the supervisee and the client. For supervisees who are beginning to see clients and who are in training this will usually mean a process recording of the session (i.e., a verbatim account of what took place in the session, written up after the session. The subject of process recordings is considered further in Chapter 5).
- getting an idea at a somewhat deeper level of thoughts and feelings that the supervisee had, about the client and when with the client, and how they feel now (the beginnings of thinking about transference and countertransference).
- allowing some joint reflection on what has gone on, and beginning to come to some provisional hypotheses about the underlying dynamics.
- helping the supervisee think about how they might work with the client in future sessions, in terms of interventions.

In addition there is of course the consideration of the special circumstances of the setting and the institution in which the counselling is situated.

Getting an account of the session with the client

The supervisor will have different expectations when it comes to reporting on the session, depending on the levels of experience and sophistication of their supervisees. While a process recording (which we will consider later in Chapter 5) might be appropriate for counsellors in training, for volunteers or complete beginners something simpler might be needed. If we think about the example of Ellie (above), and the client who presented such disturbing material, we can see that supervision of this case begins with just letting the counsellor talk about the session. You could say that there is a need for catharsis just as there is in therapy; a need to evacuate some of the unexpected and difficult feelings that the supervisee has been left with after the session with the client. And as many writers have emphasised, the experience of being able to talk freely in supervision about difficult feelings allows the supervisee to hear about those of the patient in therapy sessions (see, e.g., del Pozo (1997)).

There is a cathartic aspect to this need to talk freely, but another factor might be the desire of the supervisee to check that they are on the right lines, based on a concern to get it right with the client:

> *In supervision, Ellie wanted to know, was it ok 'just to listen'? What should she say? She needed in the first instance to say what the client had said to her and what she had replied. She had felt herself to be under great pressure – Miss C kept asking, 'why did she do it? she must have known I'd be the one who would find her'. Ellie had said, that there wasn't an easy answer to this and had then said that perhaps things would be easier in time. Miss C had expressed horror at the thought of still wanting to talk about this in three weeks' time, and Ellie had found herself saying that maybe she'd still be wanting to talk about it in three months' time or even three years' time, whereupon the client has got very upset and said she simply couldn't stand it . . . Ellie felt that she had upset Miss C unnecessarily. However at the end of the session Miss C had agreed that it might be helpful to be visited for a few months at any rate.*

Supervisees beginning work will sometimes say, 'and then I said this . . . . I don't know whether I should have done' showing their concern not only about damaging the client but also about the supervisor's reaction. The task the supervisor has is to create a working environment where what might be considered 'mistakes' by the inexperienced therapist can be talked about and understood without minimizing their importance or colluding with ways of working that are unhelpful.

Counsellors who are being supervised as part of a training can be asked to provide a process recording (verbatim report) of their sessions with clients. This has the function of enabling them to record their version of what has transpired in the session and allowing the supervisor to see something of the patient and the way in which the supervisee has responded. Process recording will be considered later in the book in more detail but it often seems that the writing of this and the reading out of the account also satisfies the need to externalise the experience of the session.

My experience and that of other supervisors I have spoken to suggests that this need to report on the session is particularly important when beginning counselling. We also remembered our own supervisions of our first clients. There could be a sense of feeling distinctly cheated, when giving one's own version of a session, if the supervisor made too many interventions before the account was finished. Trainees at this level often tend to focus on the content of the session (what was said or done) rather than the underlying process, and the next section begins to address this issue.

Thoughts and feelings about the session – reactions to the client

For some counsellors it can be quite difficult to think about their own reactions to the session. This might be because they feel this is not important, or that they should be 'neutral' in their approach. Or they think that having an opinion or a feeling amounts to making a judgement, which they feel to be wrong. Since being empathic involves an identification with the client, new counsellors sometimes take in so much of what the client feels that they lose their own sense of themselves and a separate view. This state of mind sometimes goes along with a tendency to take the client's story very literally and concretely; it takes some while to really understand the extent to which material in sessions is a reflection of the client's inner world. The supervisor's function at this point is to help the supervisee to stand back from the material. Helping the supervisee to work out what they are feeling, and what their reactions are to the narrative helps them to regain a sense of themselves.

Sometime the opposite situation occurs; the supervisee feels quite antipathetic to the client and then the need is to help the supervisee think about this situation. In the case of Ellie, it was very hard for her to admit to her initial feelings of panic and repugnance when the client so clearly needed support. Under these circumstances, supervisees sometimes find it a great relief to read Winnicott's paper (1947) 'Hate in the countertransference'; it helps them realise that in any relationship there are mixed feelings. There are also instances where supervisees, disabled by their own feelings of inadequacy and anxiety, resort to premature, over intellectual formulations of the client's difficulties.

Thinking about the emotions stirred up by the encounter also allows the supervisee to develop a more symbolic and freer way of thinking. They begin to realise that if difficulties can be thought about openly in supervision, there is less risk of them being enacted inappropriately with the client.

Reflecting on what has gone on

Given the nature and strength of the self-scrutiny in which the supervisee is often engaged, the supervisor has to decide what is the most important aspect of the work to take up with the supervisee:

In the case of Ellie, the supervisor noted that Ellie had been pulled into somewhat of an information-giving role and possibly even a somewhat retaliatory one (by emphasising the length of time it would take to get over the death) but chose instead to feed back something on the difficulty of the encounter and also pointed out that her remarks might help Miss C to realise that her difficulties were understood to be serious, and that by agreeing to continue to see Ellie, she was acknowledging the potential usefulness of the counselling. There was also some discussion as to whether Ellie felt able to go on with this work – there were other options. In other words the supervisor satisfied herself for the time being that the counsellor was not being asked to bear something outside her capacities, and that she would be able to be there for the client.

The supervisor also talked about the process going on in the session and introduced the idea that there was a connection between the feelings that Miss C was experiencing (her anger, sadness and impotence at the fact she had not been able to prevent her sister's death) and Ellie's feelings of being overwhelmed and unable to help. Miss C could not bear the feelings and by being so upset and angry in Ellie's presence she had passed some of this onto Ellie. (With a more experienced supervisee in training she would have probably talked in terms of projective identification, and its different purposes. Chapter 5 considers the subject of projective identification in more detail.)

In the above case, it was comparatively easy to understand the dynamics of the situation and Ellie's resolve was strengthened by the idea that her position was being taken seriously. She did have a choice and she chose to continue working with Miss C. What she learned from the case was the importance of letting someone express their feelings freely. After some months, the intensity of Miss C's distress abated and she could begin to think about what had gone on in her very troubled family.

Helping the supervisee think about possible interventions

As I suggested at the beginning of the chapter, trainees are often having to let go of familiar ways of working. It can be difficult for some to stay with the painful issues that a client is bringing without resorting to giving information or asking questions; I have already given the example of Linda and the dynamics that prompted her to take up this stance. Very often trainees have a natural tendency – or learn quickly – how to be reflective and empathic; what is far more difficult is to be challenging or to talk with the client about their relationship. And there are circumstances where it would be quite inappropriate for this approach to be taken with clients, either because of the remit of the agency providing the counselling or because of the experience of the trainees or the characteristics of the client. There is always a need as, for example, Thomas Ogden (1992) points out, to think about the issue of interpretation versus silent containment (p. 29). But supervisees have to develop an understanding of what is going on in psychodynamic terms, whether or not it is the right moment to say anything; being able to talk about the here and now and developing an understanding of transference/countertransference issues is a vital part of training in the psychodynamic tradition.

Some of the reluctance of supervisees to address things directly can be traced back to the concern about doing the client harm that new supervisees often have. But sometimes at the beginning, it also seems to relate to a difficulty in thinking symbolically. For example, the material may point to the fact that the client is being self-destructive in various ways, but when you talk about the matter with the supervisee they will say 'I didn't want to give the client the **idea** that I thought this was possible' as though they might be responsible for the client's actions if they verbalise something. The question of working with clients or patients who find it difficult to think symbolically is considered in Chapter 9.

Addressing these issues is another instance in which what happens in supervision can provide a model for work with clients; we need to create an atmosphere in which anything, relating to the encounter with the client, can be talked about.

The importance of the therapeutic setting

In thinking about areas for change with any particular supervisee, the supervisor needs to develop a sense of priorities. I think the first of these is to have in mind the question of whether the supervisee has created a setting where psychodynamic work can take place; if there is no bounded setting it is difficult to assess the effect of other variations in the patient's reactions of behaviour. We have already seen that a bounded setting is important in supervision too, particularly for inexperienced practitioners who have not yet developed their own sense of a bounded way of working.

It is important for supervisors to keep in mind the effects of absences, time changes and breaks on the course of work with the patient, and suggest ways of addressing these. This is particularly important for inexperienced therapists who may not have had enough of their own therapy to be aware of the impact of breaks.

A supervisee talked of her client's absences from counselling; it was diffi-cult to persuade her that they had a meaning, since the client apparently gave very good reasons for them. Some sessions later the supervisee hap-pened to mention in passing that she had had to cancel a session earlier in the work. She had apologised to the client but had not thought it necessary to explore the issue of what it meant. Although this was ini-tially denied, she felt guilty about her absence and this had prevented her thinking about the effect on the client.

In supervision, helping the supervisee maintain or re-establish the frame is always a priority, which involves thinking about how these issues might be addressed with the patient.

Summary and conclusions

For many people, their first experience of being in the role of super-visor will be of supervising counsellors and others with very little experience of working psychodynamically. We have seen that creat-ing a sense of a bounded setting allows the inevitable anxieties asso-ciated with this work to be expressed and contained. One aspect of this is that supervisors need to think about their own boundaries and recognise that changing aspects of the arrangements, although occa-sionally unavoidable, can be very disorientating for those beginning therapeutic work.

We have explored the tasks of supervision as they relate to those beginning to work with clients. The task of helping supervisees develop an increased capacity to think and reflect is of great impor-tance in allowing them to think with their clients and so give them a greater sense of containment.

The following points seem particularly relevant for those begin-ning to supervise, particularly where those being supervised are also beginners:

- Whatever our intentions, we inevitably provide a model for our supervisees in the way we set up and conduct supervision, and this is particularly true for those at the very beginning of their ther-apeutic career, where they have not internalised their own model of containment. In practice it may be very difficult to provide an absolutely secure frame, but being able to recognise when this has not been the case is very helpful to our supervisees.

- The supervisor needs to be able to engender an atmosphere where counsellors can talk honestly about their work, so that the supervisor can help them think about their own practice and interventions; those at the beginning of their careers in working psychodynamically need help in thinking about the way in which these ideas are reflected in practice.

- Learning to think psychodynamically takes time; beginners coming from other professions often fall back on former ways of relating to clients, thinking in a rather concrete way about their issues. They may also find it difficult not to over identify with their clients.

- We have to recognise that those at the beginning of their careers are inevitably anxious about their first encounters with clients or patients, and worry about doing them harm; as supervisees can also feel very burdened by the material that clients bring, supervision also has a cathartic value.

- The supervisor needs to help the supervisee provide a secure contained environment for their work; it is only when this is in place that other variations, to do with external circumstances or other aspects of the client/counsellor relationship, can be understood.

THE EMOTIONAL EXPERIENCE OF LEARNING AND TEACHING IN SUPERVISION

Introduction

In Chapter 2 we considered the particular needs of counsellors at the beginning of the supervisory relationship. I suggested that the setting created in supervision provides a framework for thinking about the complex dynamics of work with the client at a point when the supervisee is not able to provide this for themselves. This enables the supervisee to develop a capacity for containment that allows for thinking to take place in the session as well as in supervision.

Underpinning the idea of containment is the idea that learning takes place within a relationship. Alex Coren (1997), writing on thinking and development, gives a very clear account of the development of psychoanalytic thinking on the subject of containment; he expands on Bion's idea that thinking comes into play to cope with thoughts, and involves another person, who can take in, reflect on, and allow these thoughts to be re-introjected in a form which is more digestible. If we do not have someone who is receptive to our experience, however expressed, we may be forced to resort to primitive ways of managing anxiety. For young babies, these include what Freud (1911) termed 'hallucinatory wish fulfilment', for example, where the experience of hunger is denied and the child hallucinates something that substitutes for a feed, in a magical way (pp. 218–226). I suggest that the adult counterpart in supervision might be a supervisee who is unable to use (take in) what is offered in supervision, or who resorts to confusion as a defence against thinking. Both parties to supervision have a responsibility here; sometimes this situation develops as a result of a supervisor who cannot take in the nature of the supervisee's anxiety.

Certainly, what is discussed in supervision, as well as the process of supervision, has the power to make us anxious. Of course, the difficulties of the clients being considered play a large part in this, particularly where there is a danger of their harming themselves or others. But the complexities of the supervisory relationship and the nature of learning and teaching in this context can also arouse very strong feelings in both supervisee and supervisor.

This chapter therefore focuses on the supervisory couple and some of the difficulties that may arise. These difficulties include the experiential nature of supervision, and the weight of our expectations as to what supervision will involve, as well as those that arise from the educational context. The dynamics described are perhaps more likely to be activated when supervision is part of a training, where the supervisor may be responsible for teaching, monitoring and reporting on the supervisee. The formal organisational aspects of supervision for trainees at any level inevitably influence the supervisory relationship.

While we begin by thinking about problems and difficulties, we also need to consider what helps learning to take place in supervision, in terms of the responsibilities of the supervisor and supervisee.

The experiential nature of supervision

Learning about counselling and therapy from a psychodynamic perspective is bound to stir up emotional conflicts and unresolved issues, since a central tenet of this way of working is that our experience of the client – our countertransference – is an important guide to issues that the client brings to the counselling relationship. We have to allow ourselves to be vulnerable and open to the total experience of being with the client, who is likely to be in a very fragile or disturbed state of mind.

Beginning work with clients or patients and reporting on our experience means that sometimes uncomfortable aspects of our own inner worlds are brought into view, as the material is scrutinised by ourselves and our supervisor. We wonder what our supervisor's reaction will be, and how we will respond to their comments. Can the supervisor understand how difficult it is at times to think in the session, or make interventions? Are we going to be able to take in what the supervisor is saying, without being defensive or overwhelmed, and use it to find our own way of being with and helping the patient?

When we are in training, each supervision session represents a new challenge; we expect a great deal from it in terms of increasing our own understanding but we also hope to be understood. In fact we do not always know what we want; as Penelope Crick (1991, p. 237) writes, of the states of mind of students in training, 'the demands we make of a "good supervisor" are as contradictory and paradoxical as the demands familiar to the parents of adolescent children'. We need challenge, but also want kindness – structure, but also the space to make our own mistakes. We may want the security of being taught, in a more formal sense, but we also want to find our own voice in our work with clients.

Because of the subject matter, learning in psychodynamic supervision is necessarily experiential rather than simply a didactic process and can be a deeply emotional experience. Berman (2000, p. 275) considers:

> Beyond basic ideas about the setting and boundaries ... what needs to be learned is not a list of steadfast rules, but an introspective and empathetic sensitivity to the actual sources and actual impact of our actions and non actions. This is a most personal learning process that requires considerable personal exposure and is strongly influenced by the supervisory climate.

Berman is writing about the supervision of psychoanalytic candidates but I think these ideas have relevance for anyone working in the psychodynamic tradition. But the process is exposing for the supervisor too, who because of their role (or the way it is understood) may be put under different kinds of pressure to provide understanding or suggest a solution. Although the supervisor's learning is not the main task of supervision, we are inevitably learning in our role as supervisors; we elaborate our own ideas about working with patients and we also have to learn how best to help our supervisee develop as a practitioner. We have to be receptive. As Masud Khan (1972) writes '... whenever I, as a supervisor, cannot learn from a candidate's work, then he cannot learn from me either. Learning here is a mutual and reciprocal activity' (p. 118). The supervisor's learning process and its implications is not always acknowledged.

Berman (op. cit., p. 277) also draws attention to a fundamental dynamic in supervision when he writes that:

a major source of difficulty for supervisees, for example, is that the learning of new skills requires acknowledgement of their lack. And such an acknowledgment arouses shame. But in good supervision the supervisor also needs to learn and change, and at times to become aware of blind spots, or to admit not having satisfactory answers . . . .

One implication of this is that the supervisor needs to model a sense of openness and preparedness to learn. We might ask how is the supervisee expected to gain an understanding of the value and importance of remaining open to their experience if the supervisor imagines they have all the answers? At a deeper level, understanding this might mean recognising the potential in the role of supervisor for destructiveness in one form or another, for example, by being over critical of ourselves or the supervisee, having too fixed an idea of the right way of working, or enviously undermining achievements. If these issues are not thought about, they can spoil the supervisory relationship, as Robin McGlashan (2003) writes; he makes the point (p. 27) that the learning supervisor also needs containment, initially through the medium of supervision for supervision, if they are not to act (rather than reflect) in response to issues brought to sessions.

Expectations relating to supervision

Some of the emotional dynamics generated in supervision relate to unrealistic hopes, expectations and anxieties – often not conscious – of our supervisees and ourselves. Difficulties on both sides may have their origin in individual experiences and ideas about the way in which relationships should go, or they may relate particularly to supervision as a learning experience.

When we begin supervising, the strength of feelings may take us by surprise – there can be an assumption that supervision implies distance from the main emotional drama, represented by the patient or client and their difficulties; problems might be seen as residing with the patient, and not with the two people discussing the progress of the work in supervision. Or we may have a false idea of the level of experience of our supervisee, or we may idealise – or be unable to value – what we are providing in supervision. We soon discover that despite the sense of enjoyment and engagement that often characterises supervision, it can also be frustrating and at times disheartening and anxiety provoking.

A difficult beginning

The following example illustrates a difficult beginning where Robert, the supervisor, and John, the counsellor, get caught up in a powerful dynamic characterised by misunderstanding, confusion and disappointment.

Robert was a relatively inexperienced supervisor of trainee counsellors in a community counselling agency. All the trainees came from a course that Robert knew well – in fact he'd been on it himself several years earlier. He had had very positive experiences of his first supervisees, both women who had seemed to value what he had to offer and had gone on to do well as counsellors. He had been involved in assessing their competence but had found this unproblematic, since they generally conformed to his expectations.

*In his own supervision, he talked of his latest supervisee, John, and how he'd arrived at the preliminary interview on the wrong day. 'I wasn't able to see him – I suggested he come at the appointment time we'd arranged. I was taken aback when he started to argue the toss about the time – I was fairly certain I'd got it right, but was prepared to concede I'd made a mistake – but I was **sure** he was right! I was surprised how disoriented I felt by this; I wasn't prepared for an argument. I realise how much I'd taken for granted with A and M' (his previous two supervisees).*

'Anyway, he came back a week later. Once we started talking, John said that he had been turned down by his first choice of placement, which he clearly saw as more prestigious. He talked of his previous counselling experience in another context – he said he was used to working with very disturbed clients – he's had to give this up to come to us. There was a (female) supervisor there that he really admired. She's quite high up in the profession I think. I asked him about his experience of supervision. He talked about how it has been. I found myself rushing into talking about process recordings and how useful I found it when people could bring fairly detailed accounts of what had happened in the session. He was very taken aback – asked, how was he expected to remember the order in which

things were said and all that? He had never imagined that he would have to do that. Surely it was all just about his countertransference? His previous supervisor had apparently just asked him what his feelings were about the client – this was what he understood by psychodynamic supervision.'

'He has started working with clients now, but it's been an ongoing problem, the matter of the process notes. He usually brings very sketchy accounts; often says he can't remember. I get no sense of him in the room with the client – it all seems very confused, so that I feel confused too. When he does produce notes they're enormously rambling and long – by the time he's read them the supervision is nearly over – there's no time for me to contribute.'

This encounter between supervisor and supervisee highlights the influence of expectations in place before the first meeting. John comes to the interview having already experienced one rejection, and in addition he has had to give up his other placement which he seems to have enjoyed. In addition, being sent away by Robert because of the mistake over the day of his appointment may also be experienced as humiliating. We could imagine that he is feeling a sense of shame as well as anxiety – he needs a placement for his course – and that he is managing this, not very constructively, by idealizing his previous agency and subtly denigrating his possible placement with Robert. (Perhaps if the agency is no good, it will be easier to bear if he doesn't get the placement.) All in all, Robert feels as if he is told that he and his agency are second best, a status which he seems initially to accept (he is upset by the appointment day issue, seems to have little confidence that he was right about this). He feels under attack, and reasserts his authority by looking ahead to their joint task in supervision, and talking about what he expects from the supervisee. John challenges his authority; at this point it also seems as if they have quite different ideas about the **process** of supervision; as Robert commented, much later, 'Of course we both had a point – but what surprised me was the way it immediately became an issue. I really wanted to argue with him.'

As well as tensions to do with expectations, past experiences and disappointment, it seems as if there is a very competitive dynamic, introduced by John when he talks in glowing terms of the previous placement and supervisor, and Robert feels quite deskilled. They have a rather polarised view of their experiences – while John is idealising his previous placement, Robert seems to be looking back wistfully to his previous 'easier' supervisees. Perhaps he thought that supervision would always be free of conflict. The competitiveness further shows itself in an argument over what constitutes supervision, the situation perhaps being exacerbated by Robert's previous involvement with the course as a student. An interesting aspect of this encounter is that Robert seems to feel he has no choice over whether he offers the supervisee a placement. After all, one agency has refused him, and if he is already proving difficult to work with, perhaps other arrangements might suit them both. But one of Robert's personal characteristics is apparently stoicism and perhaps there is a sense of wanting to prove himself, in the eyes of the training organisation, as someone who can manage anything. Maybe he wants to triumph over the supervisor in the placement that refused John, by demonstrating his ability to manage a difficult student. The question of how to report and reflect on the work with the client seems to have become a focus for channelling conflicts over authority.

The next section considers further what might lie beneath the dynamics of these and other common experiences in supervision.

Attitudes to learning

Adult learners, including those training to work therapeutically, bring with them expectations of learning and teaching relationships which are based on much earlier life experiences. Isca Salzberger-Wittenberg, in the excellent book, *The Emotional Experience of Learning and Teaching* (1983), makes the point that any new event or change in our lives arouses ambivalent feelings. She writes, 'It is the nature of beginning that the path ahead is unknown, leaving us poised as we enter upon it between wondrous excitement and anxious dread' (p. 3). Inherent in the excitement of going into the unknown territory of a new discipline or body of knowledge is the risk of failing, in our own eyes or in those of others. I have already pointed out (Chapter 2) that it may be hard to relinquish old ways of thinking and working. Penelope Crick (1991, p. 237), writing on the experience of being supervised, reminds us of the painfulness of losing earlier versions of oneself when undergoing a training:

the task of learning itself is very difficult. We know from our clinical work how powerful the resistance to change can be, no matter how intense is the conscious striving and desire for change. When there are gains, new identifications and internalisations,

there are corresponding losses – relinquishments of earlier identifications and parts of the self. Such giving up of old ideas and
habits and ways of thinking is painful – everyone feels de-skilled
at the beginning of psychotherapy training.

There is a transference to the process of education, a process which
inevitably involves change, and a requirement to leave behind former ways of thinking and working. Freud (1914b), in his paper
'Some reflections on schoolboy psychology', comments on the emotional impact of our experience of our teachers and its effect on
interest and application to the subject being taught. He suggests
(p. 244) that a boy will, 'in the second half of childhood' detach himself from his father and transfer the ambivalent feelings – hostile and
affectionate impulses – that were originally reserved for his father
onto his teachers. The transference to learning is inevitably bound up
with our feelings about those responsible for imparting knowledge
or helping us to learn.

I have already suggested the possibility that part of the dynamic
between Robert and John above might relate to Robert's own experience of being a student; there might well be unprocessed transferences on Robert's part, to his teachers and the course, and indeed
to his own former supervisors. But it might also relate to John's
fears about the new path he has chosen. The reasons for deciding
to undertake a counselling or psychotherapy training are complex;
they relate to our own inner worlds and may relate to a need to
rework problematic issues. In some cases this reworking may take
the form of (unconsciously) evacuating or displacing our difficulties
rather than sublimating them in the service of a new professional
identity.

When the difficulties were discussed in supervision, Robert
realised that, by allowing himself to get involved in an argument,
he had become distracted from thinking about John's situation as a
counsellor at the beginning of his professional life. As he later said:

> *'I don't think I allowed for the fact that John was so anxious. I took him at
> face value, and he wanted to talk up his experience. Also I wasn't always
> able to think straight; I felt quite disoriented in our sessions – I don't
> know what contribution John himself made to this. Then again, perhaps
> it was the client I allocated him. But I think it was more about a fear of
> exposing his work to me; recently he's hinted at difficult work experi-
> ences. Training as a counsellor was meant to be a new start. I assumed
> that he was being difficult over the notes issue – but perhaps he really*

could not process what was happening at all. Things are going better now; we have been able to talk about it a little.'

Isca Salzberger-Wittenberg (op. cit.), adopting a Kleinian perspective, considers very fully the circumstances which give rise to anxiety and ambivalence in education. These are likely to be an interaction between external factors relating to the learning context as well as factors relating to our own internal worlds, often having their roots in infancy. She describes (p. 9) three main categories of anxiety; infantile feelings of being lost or confused, hopes and fears about relating to authority figures, as well as concerns about relating to other group members. (This last issue will be considered in Chapter 6.) Her examples make it clear that these areas of concern apply to adult learners, as well as to those teaching them or facilitating learning; teachers and supervisors have to bear the full force of students' expectations, hopes and anxieties as well as metabolise their own. In the example above, Robert is aware that at least three parties to the supervision – the client, the student and he himself as the supervisor – bear some responsibility for the ensuing sense of confusion.

It can be helpful to consider the particular nature of the anxieties that are affecting our supervisees, and ourselves, although often, as in the example above, different types of anxiety are interwoven.

Anxieties relating to confusion, fear of annihilation or abandonment

If supervision can engender competitive feelings on both sides, it can also at times be the setting for much more disturbing, primitive emotions and anxieties where psychic survival is at stake, panic sets in and thinking becomes impossible. We can think of this as corresponding to Klein's (1935) definition of persecutory anxiety, relating primarily to situations where the preservation of the ego is threatened (p. 269). In counsellors and therapists at the beginning of their training, this may initially manifest itself in anxieties about managing the encounter with the client. The example of Ellie in Chapter 2 seems to touch on this experience; she is initially overwhelmed by the content of the client's material, to do with the suicide of her sister but she manages to use supervision to think about her feelings of shock.

In more extreme situations, however, there is the potential for a counsellor to be quite seriously affected, almost traumatised, by an encounter with a client, not only because of the strength of the projective identification originating from the client but also because issues may relate to difficulties that have not been able to be processed sufficiently in the counsellor's own therapy or in other ways. In some instances, this results in an almost phobic avoidance of similar situations, as the following example illustrates:

Mel was a trainee counsellor, working as a volunteer at a bereavement service, and in group supervision. She'd chosen this setting because she thought that her experiences of loss and bereavement would equip her to work with clients. Her first two clients had not stayed long and she seemed unwilling to take on further clients for the time being. Her supervisor initially accepted this at face value – the other supervisees had some complicated cases to discuss, and there never seemed to be enough time. But meanwhile Mel seemed to be getting more and more diffident and nervous, worried about the supervisor's and others' reactions, and less in touch with her own abilities. The supervisor was puzzled and rather irritated; she wondered, was she really so critical and unapproachable? She was disconcerted by this attitude in herself – perhaps she needed to think about it.

The supervisor eventually took her supervision of the group to her own supervision, and became aware that actually she needed to take Mel's difficulties more seriously. She realised she had to try to understand what was going on, and set aside a private time to talk about the situation. It transpired that Mel had been very frightened by her reaction to her first client. She had realised that it reminded her of how frightened she'd been when, as a child, she had been left alone with an unfamiliar babysitter. It wasn't, she explained, that the circumstances were the same but somehow there was an unpredictable quality about her client's presentation that had touched off something and made her very anxious. She wanted to run from the room, couldn't concentrate on what he was saying, couldn't think at all. Then the client had left, perhaps because she couldn't risk saying anything very much to him, for fear of what might happen. Her feelings of fear, inhibition and failure had got out of control, to the point when the supervisor too had become a threatening figure, who would be bound to be critical. In turn the supervisor had become unsympathetic, perhaps because her own need to displace feelings of not being a helpful supervisor, or other anxieties.

The supervisor did not go into the details of Mel's early experiences; but she noted that their re-emergence in Mel's experience of the sessions had resulted in her feeling overwhelmed, powerless and passive in her attitude towards the client and also to the supervisor and to her own learning. In object relations terms, we could say that Mel feels that all her good objects have deserted her, and the difficult situation in the sessions with the clients has generalised into a state of mind where, for a while, there is no help anywhere; she is confused and cannot think. Since she is unable to let the supervisor know what is going on, and the supervisor initially cannot quite take in the degree of her anxiety, she feels that the supervisor has also abandoned her. The confusion is also a defensive reaction, in that, by allowing her to think that she is not able to take on more clients at the present, it protects her from the need to engage with the reality of work with people who might stir up such anxieties.

In this case, we might hope that being able to acknowledge the anxiety would allow Mel to take steps to think about it further, perhaps by making more use of personal therapy, if available. And perhaps it is not right for her to take further clients at the moment, if she is feeling so vulnerable. The supervisor is demonstrating, by her somewhat belated attention to the issue and her concern for Mel, that there is a place to bring these anxieties, and that it is helpful to do so since they are clearly getting in the way of working. Sometimes it needs to be pointed out in supervision that the supervisee has a responsibility to bring issues of real concern, whatever the fears about the reaction.

Anxieties relating to (internalised) authority figures

Supervision, like other activities where learning is involved, is likely to generate what we understand as Oedipal rivalries, based originally on a child's anxieties about usurping the parental position. I am thinking here of Freud's idea of the superego as developing as a reaction to the resolution of the Oedipus complex; the child solves the problem of having to relinquish the idea of the parent as their exclusive partner by identifying with the parental superego and its prohibitions. This can result in the development of a very critical stance towards both others and ourselves. As we have seen earlier in the chapter in the example of Robert and John, such anxieties may be expressed as rivalry but also as worries about failure, or struggles with taking up authority or accepting the authority of others.

Supervisees may deal with these unresolved Oedipal rivalries by becoming rather remote, distancing themselves from the clients experience, perhaps by retreating into a rather theoretical stance. Here is a rather everyday example of a trainee struggling with very critical feelings, ostensibly to do with the client, but really relating to a very demanding part of herself (superego anxieties).

Mary was seeing a first year student in her placement at a University counselling service. For various reasons, the student had found it problematic to leave home, as he felt very responsible for, and bound up with, various members of his family. He'd come to counselling preoccupied by his worries about the health and welfare of one of his parents, but it was also clear from his description, as reported, that he was at breaking point, full of feelings of loss, staying in bed all day and quite unable to engage with his course or University life.

The supervisor found that Mary's account of the sessions seemed rather sparse and somewhat lifeless; there seemed to be a mismatch between what was being described and her ability to engage emotionally with this student. Meanwhile the supervisor had the sense of an impending disaster. Mary and the supervisor agreed that Mary's somewhat cut off feelings might be something to do with the degree of depression being experienced by the student – a countertransference reaction on Mary's part, relating to depressed, hopeless feelings being projected by the student.

A few weeks later, Mary came to the session very distressed; in the previous session she had found herself getting very angry with the student and his passive, depressed way of relating, and had spoken to him very sharply. She felt very guilty and ashamed about this – the student had been upset and critical, but in any case she 'knew it wasn't right'. The supervisor found herself agreeing that this wasn't professional behaviour but she reserved judgement for the moment, thinking that perhaps it was a case of projective identification with a critical part of the student client. She asked whether Mary had any thoughts about this reaction; perhaps it was important to try and think what was going on. Mary said that her frustration had been growing; she just couldn't feel in any way sympathetic – she felt he was being 'babyish'. She then said somewhat sadly that her own experience was of having to look after herself at a much earlier age. She was shocked at having made this value judgement. The supervisor commented that Mary's experience and perhaps her capacities had been very different. Mary said, 'Yes . . . yes, I don't think I allowed for that. I think I must have thought, "what are you making so much fuss about? if I could survive so could you." Actually I did not want to think about it'.

In this case, being able to make this (emotional) connection enabled Mary to reflect on the issue and the sessions developed a more engaged, lively quality. Mary was able to use her experience to identify with the student in a more empathetic way and become less judgemental, both of the student and of herself, perhaps partly because the supervisor had been able to set aside her own judgmental feelings, demonstrating a curiosity to understand more.

In these examples we can see that trainee counsellors have to manage the inherent tension between being open to their experience, which is necessary for learning to take place, and getting into a state of mind where the feelings that are activated overwhelm them, to the point where they resort to earlier unhelpful defences against experiencing and learning. Hartung (1979), in his paper 'The capacity to enter latency in learning pastoral psychotherapy', considers how learning can best take place. He uses a developmental approach and introduces the idea of latency as a state of mind where the student is able to set aside earlier Oedipal and pre-Oedipal issues and attach themselves to a supervisor in order to learn. It involves a process of harnessing and sublimating libidinal energy, particularly in the form of curiosity, to learn skills and competencies, rather than being swayed by instinctual impulses; an implication is that the positive aspects of the transference to learning and the supervisor needs to be uppermost and both parties need to have a clear idea of their respective roles in the process of supervision. Hartung makes the point that the supervisor has a responsibility to allow this type of relationship to develop; good supervision cannot take place if the supervisor unconsciously wants to keep the supervisee at an Oedipal or earlier level of functioning, infantilising the supervisee by stressing the regressive features of the supervisory relationship. Being aware of the dynamics and the anxieties stirred up – and sometimes acknowledging them to the supervisee – is not the same as interpreting them. By this I mean that supervisors might feel they need to comment on what they observe in terms of thinking and behaviour and suggest that this needs thinking about by the supervisee – particularly if it is getting in the way of supervision. But gratuitously going into underlying factors and making links in a more interpretative way could be experienced as unbounded and intrusive by the supervisee.

This is not to suggest that difficulties in the supervisory relationship should never be talked about:

A colleague talking about her experiences of being supervised when in training, spoke of difficulties with her first supervisor, whom she considered maintained a very severe analytic attitude – as though this colleague was a patient, not a supervisee. She felt very criticised and scrutinised to the point where it was a real ordeal to present her client in supervision. One day when they were reviewing progress, she plucked up the courage to talk to her supervisor about how she felt. This made an enormous difference. As she said, 'it wasn't that the supervisor changed in any appreciable way after this discussion – but something got freed in me, because I'd been able to talk about it. I simply didn't feel constrained by her in the same way. The work became much easier as a result.'

This brief example shows something of the power of the transference but also how quickly it can be dissipated if it is addressed. In this case my colleague took responsibility for her own anxieties by addressing the situation. This will not always happen, and it is an inescapable fact of life for supervisors that there are likely to be transferences resulting in pressures put on the supervisor to take up the role of a critical parent or teacher. Sometimes the supervisor can act this out so that the trainee counsellor loses the opportunity to think about their own responsibilities in this area. This is a separate matter from the responsibilities of the supervisor for assessing the student's work and giving feedback, which also affects the dynamics. This is considered below.

Learning and educational institutions

We have discussed some of the anxieties likely to arise in supervisory situations where counsellors or therapists are in the process of training. We might ask, are these an inevitable part of learning to be a therapist? Certainly, the fact that supervisors in this context will need to report on their students' progress means that trainees may develop an expectation of their supervisors being critical and judgemental. As we have seen, supervisees may deal with this situation by devaluing what the supervisor has to offer, or by being competitive (Robert and John) by becoming detached from the emotional experience, or acting out in sessions (as with Mary) or by regressing into a confused state of mind (Mel). But supervisors' responsibility for assessment can at times result in an escalation in supervision sessions from an evaluative, reflective stance into a hyper critical approach dominated by superego anxieties.

A number of writers have drawn attention to the way in which these dynamics can pervade training institutions. The counselling and psychotherapy sector in the UK is beset by hierarchies and controversies (see, e.g., King and Randall *The Future of Psychoanalytic*

Psychotherapy (2003)). Often training standards and requirements are the focus of anxieties in organisations concerned to establish or maintain their place in the therapeutic world. A Jungian analyst, Warren Coleman, in a recent (2006) paper, 'The analytic superego', considers how these pressures can result in an unforgiving, strict approach to evaluating one's own therapeutic work and the work of others. He makes the point that these dynamics, which are based on the action of a harsh, primitive superego, pervade the profession at all levels – organisations dismissed as not offering a rigorous training make mutual recriminations against those higher up in the hierarchy. He considers that the dynamics have their origin in a 'fear of helplessness and powerlessness, especially being powerless to heal the patient's distress' (p. 101). There is a temptation to attempt to rectify this situation omnipotently by adopting a harsh view on one's own and other peoples' practice.

A prominent American psychoanalyst, Otto Kernberg, has written extensively on the way in which training institutes, because of their need to maintain a particular position in the hierarchy of organisations offering therapeutic training, may promote an inflexible attitude towards the teaching of psychotherapy. In his paper, 'Thirty methods to destroy the creativity of psychoanalytic candidates' (1996), he writes, tongue-in-cheek, 'Supervisors may carry out a crucial function in inhibiting candidates' trust in their own work and in the possibility of learning by means of their own experience' (p. 1035). He lists the ways in which this might be done, for example, by continually focussing on what the student has done wrong and indicating that advice must be followed without question. He also draws attention to the importance of supervisors and others responsible for trainings getting together to think about their approach to the work with candidates. My experience is that this is crucial for effective supervision at any level of training.

None of the forgoing consideration of the dynamics of training alters the fact that, as supervisors of counsellors in training we have to make judgements on the competence of our supervisees, and report back to them and their training institution. From time to time, we will have to fail students. This is bound to be an uncomfortable experience for the supervisor and often devastating for the supervisee. If students are likely to fail or there are areas of their work that need attention, it is important that the feedback we give is clear and unambiguous in terms of what needs to change if the supervisee's work is to be considered satisfactory. For all supervisees in training, the supervisor needs to aim for honest, clear feedback on an ongoing basis, so that there is a chance to work on areas where the supervisee is less confident before the work gets formally assessed. It is also important to point out the supervisee's strengths.

Summary and conclusions

This chapter has considered aspects of the emotional experience of entering a supervisory relationship, in particular the transferences relating to teaching and learning. Supervisees have to allow themselves to abandon old ways of thinking and acting and become open to new experiences both in their work with clients and in supervision. Supervisors also learn in supervision. We have seen that this generates anxiety at a number of levels; often Oedipal rivalries and uncertainties will emerge in the supervisory relationship, and this may make it difficult for the supervisor to take up their role. Anxiety at a more fundamental, persecutory level, often relating to feeling overwhelmed and confused by the nature of the client's material, can also spill over into supervision. We have also thought about the nature of the defences that supervisees resort to under these circumstances; for example, they may become competitive, become emotionally detached or become confused and deskilled.

Points to note for supervisors include:

- Although the roles of supervisor and supervisee are different, both parties need to have an open attitude to learning from the experience of thinking together about the clients or patients. This is a further example of the importance of the supervisor modelling a thoughtful and reflective stance.
- We need to keep in mind the strength and nature of the anxiety that engaging in work with clients and bringing them to supervision can engender, as well as the ways in which this might express itself, and be defended against.
- Supervisors have to be aware of these issues while fostering a cooperative learning environment where the strengths of the supervisee can be drawn upon and appreciated. While difficulties in learning might result in a regressed or defiant attitude on the part of the supervisee, it is important not to infantilise the supervisee.

- Such difficulties are likely to become more dominant when the supervisee is also a trainee; training institutions also play their part in contributing to students' anxiety. Supervisors can mitigate this by making sure that the feedback they give is clear and unambiguous and allows time for supervisees to see what they need to think about, in order to pass the course.

THEORY AND SUPERVISION

Introduction

This chapter considers the contribution that psychodynamic theories – both about counselling and psychotherapy and about aspects of supervision – can make to our practice as supervisors. In supervision, as in psychotherapy, theory can provide a containing framework for the supervisor and the supervisee to think about the complexities of events in sessions. As readers will be aware from Chapter 1, theory in this context means the psychoanalytic theory on which psychodynamic thinking is based. In addition, there is a growing body of theory which has developed in relation to the complex tasks of supervision, often involving a more systemic way of thinking, as well as models which consider the needs of supervisees at different levels of experience.

Theory provides a structure for our thinking but it also has to be recognised that an over reliance on particular theories can be defensive, and result in losing sight of the patient or client, and the responsibility of the therapist and supervisor. We cannot be too rigid – sometimes we can make theory into a straitjacket rather than a container. In addition both supervisors and supervisees have their own, often unrecognised, theories which may be a hindrance to understanding.

Intra-psychic theories – focussing on the patient

Theories relating to supervision are inevitably bound up with changing ways of thinking about psychotherapeutic theory and practice. The early contributions to psychoanalytic thought emphasised intra-psychic processes rather than aspects of the relationship between therapist and patient. When Freud first developed theories about his patients, he was concerned to understand the thoughts and conflicts, conscious and unconscious, that lay behind the various distressing symptoms for which they sought his help. As he (1893–1895, p. 139) wrote in the case history of Elisabeth Von R.:

I arrived at a procedure which I later developed into a regular method and employed deliberately. This procedure was one of clearing away the pathogenic psychical material layer by layer, and we liked to compare it with the technique of excavating a buried city . . . . The whole work was, of course, based on the expectation that it would be possible to establish a completely adequate set of determinants for the events concerned.

The main concern was therefore to discover information about the patient's past which had been lost to consciousness and make links between events in the past and the present difficulties. It was thought that undoing the repression which had led to the formation of the symptoms would render them unnecessary, the assumption being that they had only come into being as a disguised expression of conflict. Freud had recognised the transference – the feelings that the patient might show for the doctor, relating to past figures in their life – very early on in his career, but it was generally considered to be a sign of resistance which got in the way of the patient's understanding of their difficulties.

Equally, since it was thought that the analyst should be as neutral as possible, the idea took hold that any feelings the analyst might have towards the patient (countertransference) were seen as something to be dealt with by the analyst and overcome rather than thought about in the context of the treatment and the patient; they were a sign that the analyst needed to think further about his own tendencies and blind spots. This may help to account for the fact that, in the beginning, the analyst's own training analysis was generally thought to be the best place to explore difficulties in working with patients.

Developments: object relations and countertransference

As psychoanalytic thinking developed, new ways of conceptualizing the structure and the dynamics of the mind came into being, starting with Freud's development of the structural model of the mind, and the formulation of the idea of ego, superego and id (see, e.g., his account in the New Introductory Lectures 'The Dissection of the Psychical Personality'). He introduced the idea of one part of the mind observing another – as he writes (1933, p. 59), 'the ego can take itself as an object, treat itself like other objects, can observe itself, criticize itself.... In this, one part of the ego is setting itself over against the rest.' In the same lecture he also makes the point that as the child's ego develops, identifications are made with aspects of parental and other significant figures. This model allowed for the development of the concept of internal objects, ways of representing the patient's thoughts and feelings, conscious and unconscious, about parts of the self and others.

These ideas were taken up in different ways by Klein and Winnicott and others and led to the development of the body of theories based on object relations. The focus on the patient's internal objects also involved thinking about the **processes** by which the patient related to his objects, both internal and their representatives in the outside world. Readers wanting a description of Klein's thinking will find an accessible account in her (1959) paper, 'Our adult world and its roots in infancy'. Concepts that are part of the thinking of most counsellors working in the psychodynamic tradition, such as splitting, projection, identification and projective identification, were developed to describe different ways of relating and this also gave more scope for the relationship between analyst and patient to be brought into focus. In particular, it began to be realised that the effect of the transference on the therapist (countertransference) could be used to understand the patient.

Paula Heimann, in her ground-breaking paper on countertransference, set out the idea that the concept of analytic neutrality had been taken too far, with the result that student analysts believed that any kinds of emotional reaction towards a patient should be suppressed. In her paper, 'On counter-transference' (1950), she stated that, on the contrary, 'the analyst's emotional response to his patient within the analytic situation represents one of the most important tools for his work. The analyst's counter-transference is an instrument of research into the patients unconscious' (p. 81). In particular, the countertransference represented the (initially) unconscious reaction of the analyst to the patient's material and provided a check on the understanding gained from the more verbal, manifest content of the patient's communication. As she (op. cit., p. 82) wrote,

> The aim of the analyst's own analysis, from this point of view, is not to turn him into a mechanical brain which can produce interpretations on the basis of a purely intellectual procedure, but to enable him to sustain the feelings which are stirred in him, as opposed to discharging them (as does the patient) in order to

subordinate then to the analytic task in which he functions as the patient's mirror.

If an analyst tries to work without consulting his feelings, his interpretations are poor. I have often seen this in the work of beginners, who out of fear, ignored or stifled their feelings.

So it came to be accepted that the therapist's feelings, far from being an obstacle to be analysed away, could be used to further the understanding of the patient. The term 'countertransference' tends to be used now to describe the totality of feelings, thoughts and impressions of the therapist; of course this does not take away from the need to be constantly examining one's reactions, and their relation to personal issues and tendencies as well as to the patient. (Psychoanalysts working in the classical tradition may continue to use countertransference to mean the therapist's transference onto the patient.)

Very often, countertransference relates to a feeling that is initially disavowed by the client, and experienced by the counsellor through the mechanism of projective identification. This will be a common experience for many readers.

A simple example that came to my mind is that of a student that I was counselling, who was having great difficulty in finishing off a dissertation. He was full of energy, and plans and ideas for ways of accomplishing this, and as he talked I became more and more uncertain and eventually rather depressed. I ceased to believe that he would complete this project – and then realised that he had little hope that he would finish the work. When I raised the idea that perhaps he found it hard to believe at times that he would succeed, he repudiated the idea at first, but gradually recognised that he had been trying to forget about the possibility of failure. This thought allowed him to be more realistic about his plans and he did eventually complete the work.

This seems to be an example of projective identification used not only to get rid of some difficult thoughts – the student's idea that he might fail – but also as a means of communication, an idea developed by Bion in his paper, 'A theory of thinking' (1962). The student had after all come to get some help with his difficulties and although he had not initially been able to put these precisely into words, he had communicated something very powerful to me as the listener.

Many writers have contributed to thinking on countertransference and projective identification and some of the ideas relating to these subjects will be considered in the context of the process of supervision (Chapter 5). The concept of projective identification is a complicated one, since it is used in different ways; those wanting a clear description of the various ways in which this term can be used might find Elizabeth Bott Spillius's (1992) account helpful.

Theories about supervision – the contribution of Harold Searles

The idea of countertransference as an aid to understanding also led to a reappraisal of the dynamics that might be operating in supervision, which by this stage had become a separate part of a candidate's training. In a paper titled 'The informational value of the supervisor's emotional experiences' (1955), Harold Searles, a psychoanalyst working in the USA, wrote of the way in which the dynamics of the therapist–patient interaction are often reflected in the supervisory relationship. Supervisors had thoughts and feelings that they should take seriously. As he wrote (p. 158):

> In my view, the supervisor experiences, over the course of a supervisory relationship, as broad a spectrum of emotional phenomena as does the therapist or even the patient himself – although to be sure, the supervisor's emotions are rarely so intense as those of the therapist and usually much less intense than the patient. Moreover the supervisor can often find that these emotions within himself do not represent foreign bodies, classical countertransference phenomena, but are highly informative reflections of the relationship between therapist and patient.

Searles thought that the reflection process (now usually called 'parallel process') was a vital aid to understanding something that might have been missed in the account of the session brought by the supervisee. The supervisor's emotional reactions were a result of the therapist's unconscious identification with a part of the patient that could not be expressed adequately in words and therefore needed to be communicated through other means. But he did not think of this phenomenon as something that was always present, nor that it was necessarily a good idea to share the thought directly with the supervisee, finding that it was more productive to express the insights gained in this way in terms of what was going on for the patient. Although he thought that the dynamics of the reflective process would be more likely to occur with inexperienced supervisees, he considered that they were always a possibility, particularly when a therapist was intensely anxious about his patient. He recognised the possibility that the process might originate with the supervisor or the therapist, as well as the patient.

The idea of a link between the dynamics of the relationship of the patient with the therapist and later events in supervision has been very widely taken up by those thinking and writing about supervision. As with any theory, if pursued to its logical conclusion, this approach can result in the exclusion of other ways of thinking, and a loss of the sense of the complexity of what might be going on. This is a point made by Michael Jacobs (1996, p. 63) who comments that:

> too often 'parallel process' is used to describe things that are staring the supervisory couple in the face.... In practice too we must note that such perceptions occupy only a *small* part of supervisory hours, although when they occur they offer clues to obscure yet highly relevant areas which trouble the patient-therapist relationship.

The following example illustrates a situation where a parallel process does seem to be operating:

> *A supervisee in training presented a patient, Mr B, whom she had been working with for nearly a year. Her work with the patient, who was demanding and imperious in various ways, had been thoughtful and painstaking. After the Christmas break, the patient had missed two out of the first three sessions. The supervisee was at her wits' end – things were going badly wrong in her patient's life, often because the patient provoked very strong reactions in other people. He had previously told her that he was likely to get sacked from his job and that his relationship was breaking down. The therapy sessions were dominated by the outside realities of his life, which were seen to be completely beyond his control.*
>
> *The supervisee presented an account of the only session he had attended in a mood of desperation. There was a sense of everything collapsing and the therapy being dismissed as irrelevant or even burdensome – at the very time when things were at their worst, the patient was missing sessions. The supervisor thought that the supervisee needed to make links to get the patient to think about the way in which he was dismissing the therapy as a possible source of help – and since*

the supervisee seemed so stuck, suggested various ways this could be brought into the sessions, linking it to his anger about his abandonment over the break and so on. Every time he made a suggestion, the supervisee responded, sadly at first and then with a barely disguised irritation, with the idea that saying that would be out of the question – or else that she had said that, but no notice had been taken. 'He's so fragile – he will leave – he'll be furious if I say that – it will be quite counter productive' – were among the responses to the supervisor's suggestions.

The supervisor felt quite cast down, surprisingly so, by the way in which his comments has been apparently rejected out of hand. As he later said 'I realised I was probably being far too directive – more so that usual. I was trying too hard to help. I stopped for a moment and found myself saying "I think you've just got to bear being a bad object at the moment". I hadn't consciously thought of this but of course this came out of my own gradual acceptance that I was being experienced as a bad object by my supervisee – or at least a not very helpful one.'

The supervisee had accepted ruefully that there was no easy way of saying something which would be seen as helpful to this patient. What then developed was a more constructive discussion where both supervisee and supervisor made an effort to think more freely, playing with various ideas about the patient. The supervisee said that, surprising as it might seem, she was actually very fond of this patient – perhaps she hadn't done him justice when describing him. The supervisor realised that he had been somewhat harsh in his insistence that certain points had to be got across – perhaps the patient was very far from being able to hear them. He began to think of the patient as vulnerable rather than simply difficult – something he'd inadvertently lost sight of, partly because of his own unacknowledged feeling that he was finding the supervisee difficult.

In the next supervision, the supervisee reported that she had found the courage to address some of these issues with the patient and that he had seemed relieved.

In this example, we can see that something is being acted out which the participants seem to feel cannot be expressed adequately in words. It is not enough for the patient to tell the supervisee (in the role of therapist) how wrong and useless everything seems, although the supervisee is apparently sympathetic. It has to be acted out through the missed sessions and through the hopeless, accusatory tone with which the patient expressed his concerns. But similarly the supervisee seems to feel that she is not being heard in supervision; she conveys the idea that the supervisor hasn't at all grasped the idea of what is it like being with this man who is so distressed and angry. Her comments, although expressed in a softened form, feel like a complaint, as far as the supervisor is concerned. He feels chastened and then a sense that he is trying to do something impossible, that nothing he says will be of any use. After some reflection, he is able to use these feelings to understand that something very powerful is being conveyed about the interaction between the patient and the supervisee.

Searles's ideas represent the beginning of a systemic way of looking at events in the supervisory relationship, in the sense that what happens in one area – the sessions with the patient – affects another relationship, the supervisory relationship. Other writers have considered the systemic element from a different point of view, developing theories on the effect of the supervisory relationship on that of the supervisee as therapist/patient. Robert Langs is prominent among these writers.

The supervisor's influence – Robert Langs

We have already considered Langs' contribution to supervision in terms of his views on the need to maintain a consistent frame for supervision. A related strand of his thinking focuses on ways of understanding the deeper unconscious meaning of the material that the patient brings (see, e.g., his book (1994) *Doing Supervision and Being Supervised* which sets out aspects of his theory and recommendations for practice in some detail). He advocates a very structured approach to supervision, with the supervisee always working from a process recording and the supervisor intervening according to particular criteria, when it is considered the supervisee has failed to make a correct intervention. This allows for both the supervisor and the supervisee to see the effects of their interventions.

Langs considers that the patient is very finely attuned to changes in the setting and to discordant events in the therapy and that these will always emerge in the material, acting as confirmation when the supervisor has made a correct formulation of the difficulties in the patient/therapist relationship. But he makes the point that this is also true of breaks in the frame on the part of the supervisor – there will be evidence – whether presented as material from the patient, or in the form of acting out in the patient/therapist relationship – of the effect of such deviations from good practice.

*We have already considered the example of the supervisee who altered his session time with the client, shortly after I had cancelled a session with him (Chapter 2). In this case I was alerted to the possible effect my cancellation had had by the supervisee reporting that the patient hadn't turned up, which he was surprised at, as he had altered the time to suit the client. It is clear that my breaking the frame allowed the supervisee to think that it was helpful to alter the frame with the client, if this was requested. But we can take the argument further, according to Langs' model; this example also shows the way in which the client's behaviour acts as a check on the practice of the supervisor, as well as the supervisee. Although **consciously** grateful for the time change, the client had in fact found it disturbing at an unconscious level, as the missed session and other material from the subsequent session showed. The client's sensitivity to these events becomes a source of information for the supervisee (and especially for me as the supervisor) on the effects of altering the setting.*

We have seen that both Langs and Searles introduce a systemic element into thinking about supervision, in that events in one setting influence in various ways what happens in the other setting. Searles focuses mainly on the influence of the patient/therapist dyad on the supervisory couple, whereas Langs, with his preoccupation with the importance of maintaining the therapeutic frame in supervision, considers how deviations from good practice on the part of the supervisor and the therapist are reflected in the patient's material or actions. Casement (1985, 1990) elaborates on this latter theme in some detail, showing ways in which the patient's material is a means of understanding and monitoring the therapist's effectiveness.

Intersubjectivity

So far we have considered the dynamics in terms of two sets of pairs and their interactions. There is of course an implied third pair, the supervisor and the client or patient. While the patient may not consciously know of the supervisor's existence, the effects of the supervisor's thoughts about, and identifications with, the patient may be transmitted via the supervisee.

Some recent contributions see all three of those involved in the therapy/supervision as linked in a relational matrix. These ideas have their basis in the ideas of the relational school of psychoanalysis and the belief that therapeutic relationships are co-constructed and effectively take on a life of their own. As Susan Howard (2007, p. 72) puts it, describing this approach:

> Not only does the therapist become a full partner rather than an observer in the construction of the therapeutic relationship, but also the supervisor becomes a full partner rather than an observer in the construction of the supervisory relationship. Consequently the minds of all three participants (patient, supervisee and supervisor) are understood to contribute to the process of supervision, including enactments. Thus all three are the subject of reflection and discussion in supervision.

One implication of the model is that more space is given to allowing the unconscious thoughts of the supervisor and supervisee to emerge in supervision, resulting initially in a move away from a focussed discussion about the patient. Brown and Miller (2002) give an account of a situation where this initial move to a more 'free associating' and personal discussion of themes on the part of the supervisee and supervisor eventually allowed some good work to be done with a patient where the therapy seemed struck – in the course of the process, some aspects of the dynamic of the therapeutic relationship, which was to do with difficulties in entering the adult world, became apparent and so the therapy could move on.

In the case illustrated by Brown and Miller, it seems as if freeing up the supervisor and supervisee to think around the subject allowed some creative thinking to happen, which they could then apply to the entrenched situation in which the patient found himself. There is a more active exploratory process going on in supervision, and the patient is left on one side for a while. Whether this is helpful in all circumstances seems uncertain; I would suggest that, as with many systemic models of supervision, such dynamics can be more clearly seen when one patient is being exclusively discussed in supervision on a regular basis. This situation allows for a more consistent setting against which the subtleties of the various interactions can be seen more clearly.

Where does all this leave the supervisor? It seems that the theories presented express something of the tensions inherent in supervision. One such tension might be between a school of thought that wants a structured and (apparently) more task-orientated way of working in supervision, and another which emphasises a more free-floating attention, allowing the material from the session to sink in and understanding to develop. This tension is there for every supervisor; in our teaching capacity we have an idea of what supervisees need to learn and sometimes we can find ourselves getting didactic, needing – and sometimes wanting – to emphasise points about the patient and the supervisee's interventions. But we also want to show, by example and attitude, that we take into account the unconscious, ours and the supervisee's as well as the patient's. This can only be done by creating a situation where there is space for thoughts and feelings to emerge, in a more reflective, free-floating way.

Developmental models of supervision – focussing on the supervisee

In Chapter 2 we considered the needs of counsellors beginning supervision and there are a number of models which acknowledge the needs of the supervisee at different stages of their development as counsellors or therapists. One such model is that of Hawkins and Shohet (2000) who suggest four main developmental stages (pp. 60–64). These are considered below:

Level 1 – self centred

When beginning work with clients, the supervisee is anxious and very dependent on the supervisor's approval. This may be partly because the supervisee is being evaluated (see Chapter 3) but also because, realistically, the supervisee knows that they do not have the experience to evaluate their own progress and performance, so are dependent on the supervisor's judgement. This may initially mean that there is less space in the supervisee's mind to think about clients:

The example of Ellie (Chapter 2) and her anxieties about saying the right thing to a traumatised client when she herself was feeling so over-whelmed with the material presented, seems to illustrate this point. It is difficult for her to think of the client – she feels quite disabled in the session and, initially, in supervision, by her own worries. We have already considered that the structure of supervisory provision, in terms of boundaries, is important in giving beginners a sense of containment. A more didactic style of teaching is appropriate and might help to allay anxieties. Hawkins and Shohet also point to the need for positive feedback and encouragement.

Level 2 – client centred

Hawkins and Shohet see this level as involving an oscillation, between being quite dependent on support, and a somewhat premature autonomy. This can sometimes be linked to an over identification with the client, with the supervisor being pushed away. They liken this stage to an adolescent state of mind, where parental figures (in this case, the supervisor) are either idealised or thought to be inadequate in various ways.

Some supervisees challenge the supervisor's authority and methods of working very directly. The example of Robert and John in Chapter 3 is an illustration of this; we saw that eventually Robert, the supervisor, realised that John's bravado covered a great deal of anxiety. This was really only understood once work had started; John presented his sessions with his first client very defensively, tending to resort prematurely to theoretical explanations as a way of avoiding staying with the patient's difficulties. But then when challenged he could suddenly lose all sense of himself in the sessions, attributing his confusion to the client, and wanting to know what to do. At this stage in his development it was very difficult for him to find a middle position, accepting that he might have some strengths but that he still had a lot to learn.

Level 3 – process centred

Supervisees at this level are considered more confident and autonomous, more able to adjust their way of working to the particular client being seen. They are able to be with the client in the session and at the same time have an overview of what might be going on in process terms. (Hawkins and Shohet (op. cit., p. 62) call these abilities 'helicopter skills'.) The trainee has incorporated their theoretical knowledge into their practice in such a way that it becomes part of them rather than a series of learned commands. (I would conceptualise this in terms of being able, in the normal course of events, to let go of the more excessive prohibitions of the superego in terms of learning (Chapter 3).) Supervision becomes more collegial.

The supervisee working with Mr B, whose anger and distress was shown by his missing sessions (described earlier in the chapter) might be thought to be able to work at this level. Although initially both supervisee and supervisor are unable to develop their thoughts about what is happening in the session with the patient, they get to a point of understanding in the end and are able to think together and develop a fuller picture of the patient.

Level 4 – process in context centred

This level is one where knowledge has been consolidated and deepened through integration of theory and practice. (Hawkins and Shohet describe this in terms of knowledge becoming wisdom.) But it is also about taking account of the wider context of the work with clients and patients and being able to move flexibly from one point of view to another. Implicit in this level of working is a sense of being able to tolerate uncertainly and confusion while still being able, most of the time, to think about the situation.

Hawkins and Shohet point out that supervisors too are passing through developmental stages, and emphasise that individuals should not start practising supervision until they themselves, as practitioners, have reached the process centred stage. Certainly supervisors need to have integrated their understanding of their own theoretical knowledge with their work as a practitioner.

The developmental approach is attractive in that it is relatively simple and makes intuitive sense. It is the approach adopted implicitly if not more explicitly by many training courses; the criteria for progress made often reflect expectations at different stages of development as counsellors or therapists. We would not expect a student just beginning to work with clients to have grasped the subtleties of the transference; they need to get used to being with the client and learning to listen and intervene appropriately, to tolerate silence and the strength of feelings being expressed in the client's material.

Like any framework, the developmental approach can constrain thinking. And sometimes we and our supervisees will feel that no progress is being made or learning can't be consolidated. All sorts of circumstances, internal and external, can result in the supervisee temporarily losing sight of their strengths and competence. This is also true for supervisors; a patient in crisis, a challenging situation or changes in personal circumstances can also result in a sense of inadequacy, a lack of attention or enactments of various kinds. Perhaps what distinguishes supervisors functioning at Level 4 is a sense that whatever happens there will eventually be something that can be learned from the situation, no matter how painful.

Functions of theory in relation to supervision

There are a number of ways in which theory comes into the supervision process, related to various functions or tasks of supervision; these are outlined below.

Using our knowledge of theory to help the supervisee understand the client

Part of the educative function of supervision is to help the supervisee to develop a more elaborated and sophisticated idea of theory in relation to their practice as a counsellor. When we are in training, we learn about theory in outline but it is the process of relating it to everyday situations as well as to therapeutic work which makes it come alive. In fact we could say that this is a continuous process if we are to be alive to the experience of being with our patients or clients.

The supervisee needs to gain an understanding of the client and their circumstances, both externally and in terms of their internal world and to make links with the theories they have been taught. This means paying attention to the way in which the client uses the counselling, including exploring the meaning of, for example, missed sessions and lateness. Developing the skills of listening to the client's narrative and formulating hypotheses, however partial and tentative, as to what lies behind their concerns, allows the supervisee to become increasingly confident of their ability to think psychodynamically.

This process needs to be led by the client's material; of course, it is also important to model a sense of openness and a willingness to revise ideas. In this aspect of supervision, our relationship with the theory from our own training, and the way in which we have made it our own, is a very important aspect of our effectiveness as a supervisor. Supervisors also benefit from remembering their own learning experiences, and how long it takes to integrate theory with practice.

In this context, we need to be aware of the assumptions lying at a deeper level behind our own use of theory, and of those of our supervisees. Masud Khan (1972, p. 118), writing about supervision and the need for mutual learning, makes the point that:

> every candidate has his own 'theory' but is not intellectually aware of it. The task of the supervisor is to help the student to

become aware of his crude and tentative theory and explore and examine it in the light of what others have done before and made available to us.

My experience of working with counsellors at the beginning of their professional life suggests that very often they place a great value on knowing all about the client's past history and present circumstances. This can sometimes be behind the tendency for new counsellors to ask too many questions. Curiosity is of course a useful and necessary characteristic for a therapist, but sometimes it seems as if the underlying theory is that knowledge is everything; if links can be made between past and present, insight will follow and problems will be solved. In a sense, supervisees at this point are thinking rather as Freud did when he first worked with his hysterical patients; if the meaning of symptoms could be found, then they would vanish and the patient would be cured. Freud discovered very quickly that it was not as simple as that. In his paper (1914a), 'Remembering, repeating and working through', he writes of the resistance that accompanies patients' discoveries about their unconscious motives, and how this can be expressed by the compulsion to repeat, in the transference. Patients need to work through such resistance before they can make changes, and this is often a long process. Those beginning to work therapeutically often need reminding that change at a profound level will take time. This is also important for us to remember when we are supervising; when the material being presented is unfocussed or confusing, we need to remind ourselves that a premature striving after understanding can be unproductive.

Helping the supervisee think about the relationship with the client

The supervisee needs help in thinking about what has transpired in a session, in terms of what the client is trying to communicate emotionally, and the effect this had on the supervisee, in terms of their response. The theories I find useful in this context are those that allow an examination of the process between the client and the counsellor, in particular aspects of transference and countertransference, and associated phenomena such as projective identification, and ways in which concerns can be enacted rather than expressed in words. This aspect of supervision calls for the supervisor to be in touch with their own emotional reactions to the material and their ability to free associate to it. Such understanding eventually needs to be expressed in terms of possible interventions/interpretations in future sessions with the client.

Allowing the supervisor to think, psychodynamically, about the relationship between themselves and the supervisee

Theories which are helpful in this context might include the idea of the developmental level that the supervisee has reached, as outlined above, as well as theories emphasising the systemic nature of supervision. When things seem to be going wrong, misunderstandings developing or impasses appearing in supervision, theories about parallel process allow the possibility to be considered that perhaps some of the disturbance originates from the client/patient. When this is true, drawing the parallels can help both supervisor and supervisee to recognise areas where changes need to be made without getting too enmeshed in their own relationship. But it does not take away from the necessity and responsibility to think about other possibilities. Chapter 3 has considered the emotional experience of learning in supervision and highlighted some likely dynamics, including rivalry and challenges to authority. And some of these may originate with the supervisor – there may be envious feelings about the competence or other qualities shown by the supervisee which have to be acknowledged implicitly.

Using these theories to think about process does not imply that supervisors always need to share their thoughts with supervisees. Indeed, this can be a distraction and a burden, particularly for counsellors at the beginning of their training. But it does mean taking the time to understand the idiosyncratic nature of the relationship and the way in which both supervisor and supervisee can be pushed into enacting an unrecognised dynamic, because of what each stirs up for the other.

Helping the supervisor think about and define the boundaries and functions of supervision

These include theories relating to the type of relationship that can exist between the supervisor and supervisee, for example the question of the way in which supervision differs from therapy, the need for practical help in particular circumstances and the question of the supportive function of supervision. We have briefly thought about some of these ideas in Chapter 1. Again, these theories provide a background for the supervisor, allowing a consideration about the setting and responsibilities of supervision. These issues need to be addressed more explicitly when boundaries are threatened.

The functions of supervision will be illustrated further in the next chapter which considers the process of supervision. Subsequent chapters consider theories relevant to the context in which supervision takes place.

Summary and conclusions

This chapter has traced the development of theories which have impacted on supervision, and shown that thinking about supervision has been very much influenced by prevailing psychoanalytic theories. A hundred years ago, the focus was on the patient and what analysis could discover about their internal conflicts. Now, although we are of course still concerned with helping the patient to understand themselves, we have different ways of looking at the process of therapy, and of using the interaction between the patient and the therapist as a source of information about the patient. The fact that interactions between patient and therapist have become a focus for study has led to a re-examination of the process of supervision and the way in which dynamics in this setting may reflect those in the therapeutic setting and vice versa. In addition, we have considered the developmental perspective taken by some writers and look at some of the examples from this and other chapters in the light of this approach.

Finally I look at the different functions that theory can have for the supervisor, in terms of its usefulness in describing or illuminating the therapeutic and supervisory relationship. When we think about the role of theory in supervision, a number of points emerge:

- Theory provides a framework that helps us make sense of what is going on in both therapy and supervision; however, privileging one theory to the exclusion of others can limit our thinking. In supervision as in therapy, theory needs to be at the back of our mind and integrated to the point where it can contain and underpin the work of supervision without dominating it.
- One implication of this is that supervisors need to have developed to a point in their career where their theoretical understanding is well integrated into their own practice as counsellors and psychotherapists.

- Writers on the subject of supervision place differing emphases on the need for structure and a precise methodology in supervision, as opposed to a less defined, more free-floating way of looking at the material. Adopting one way of working rather than another might be a matter of temperament and preference as well as of relating to the particular needs of our supervisees.
- Supervisees and supervisors also have their own implicit theories which need to be discovered and examined.

THE PROCESS OF
SUPERVISION

Introduction

In Chapter 4, I outlined a number of theoretical approaches to supervision in the psychodynamic tradition. We have seen that these have followed developments in psychoanalytic thinking; in particular developments in thinking about transference and countertransference have led to the developments of theories relating specifically to supervision and the way in which the dynamics of supervision are influenced by what is going on in sessions with the patient, and vice versa.

The aim of this chapter is to consider in more detail what the ideas discussed so far might mean in practice; how do we go about doing supervision, once arrangements have been set up? There are many factors that will influence what happens in any supervision session, including the ways in which the client or patient, supervisee and supervisor interact, as well as external factors such as the context in which the therapeutic work is being carried out. In addition, we all have our own experiences of being supervised and will have developed an implicit model, which will relate to our own ideas on the purpose of supervision, and the theories we have found helpful in our own therapeutic work. Where do we start?

When we considered the importance of establishing a framework for supervision in Chapter 2, I also outlined four basic tasks of supervision. Briefly, they are:

- getting an account of what has transpired between the supervisee and the client
- getting an idea at a deeper level of thoughts and feelings that the supervisee had, about the client, both in the session and afterwards (including in supervision)

- reflecting on what has gone on (which involves thinking about the underlying dynamics of the session and what this indicates about the client)
- in the light of this understanding, helping the supervisee think about how they might work with the client in future, in terms of possible interventions

The way in which we think about these tasks relates to the level of experience of the individual supervisee, their strengths and weaknesses and the way in which they react to us. In this context, the 'actual' relationship between supervisor and supervisee, particularly the degree of trust established, becomes important. In addition, as Chapter 4 has highlighted, there is a complex systemic relationship between the client/counsellor interaction and that of the supervisor/supervisee; the experience of both participants in the supervision session can give us information, among other things, about the client/counsellor interaction. The question of the wider context is one which will be considered in more detail in Chapter 7.

Getting an account of the session with the client

How can we best begin to understand what has gone on in the session between the counsellor and the client? Counsellors and therapists in training within the psychodynamic tradition are usually expected to bring and read out a 'verbatim' report (process recording) based on their memory of the session. The nature of this is ambiguous; it can never be a true, verbatim account of everything that is said in a session, unless it is a typed transcript of the session – which is not what is wanted, for a variety of reasons. In purely practical terms, listening to a transcript would allow no time for the content to be processed, as well as raising ethical problems to do with privacy and confidentiality. The supervisee needs to have written down an account of their memory of the session, since what we are interested in is their experience.

In introducing new supervisees to the subject of process recordings I find it helpful to let them know that I do not expect them to remember every detail, that the important thing is to get an idea of the main themes with as much as they can remember of what the client said and what their responses were, in the order in which this happened. It is useful if they note how they felt and thought about what took place but this will probably come up at some stage in the supervision anyway. I also say that it is very useful to note anything that happened or was said on the time boundary of the session.

Writers on supervision differ in the importance they accord to the process recording. Robert Langs (1994) has given very detailed and precise information about what he expects of the supervisee's written notes, and indeed at what point the supervisor should intervene; other writers point out that sometimes the process recording can seem like a straitjacket of earlier page and they prefer a more free-flowing account of the session. However, for those in training, there are a number of advantages to writing up a full verbatim account of sessions. It encourages an attention to the language, the actual words used in the encounter, which allows the feel of the session to be set down in a lively way. It also encourages the supervisee to focus on their own interventions, as well as what the client said, and allows them to explore the effects of these in supervision. And, as Langs points out, it allows the supervisor to check whether their tentative hypotheses about the patient have any validity; if we are in touch with the patient being presented, through the medium of the supervisee, there will be moments when our comments anticipate a dynamic which is then confirmed by events later in the session.

Another merit of the process recording is that the supervisee has already begun, in the process of writing up the session, to digest the contents of the interaction and to reflect on what has gone on, and this will shape the way in which they present the material and gives the supervisor an idea of some of the emerging themes. In apparently describing the manifest content of the session, the supervisee's unconscious is already working on the material. But there is a paradox; we ask people to remember as much as they can, in the knowledge that the account will always be incomplete, and that another person would bring out different aspects of the encounter. As Thomas Ogden (2005) writes, almost as an aside, in describing a particular supervisory experience: 'When I quote the patient's words, I am of course not quoting the patient but quoting Dr M's "fiction" derived from his conscious and unconscious experience with the patient.'

Langs (op. cit.) makes the point that when writing notes, supervisees will often select material that reveals errors and frame breaks, because of a (largely unconscious) need to confess to the supervisor, stemming from guilt. My experience of supervisees' presentations has borne this out; I think of it as related to the way in which supervisors almost inevitably represent a superego function at points in a training – indeed, sometimes long after it has finished (see Chapter 3). Supervisees in this state of mind will sometimes say: 'and then I said . . . . of course once I said it I realised that wasn't right . . . .' Some of these comments might indicate a desire to pre-empt any criticism on the part of the supervisor. But I think often it shows a wish to build a trust in the supervisor as well as to think about more appropriate interventions. It can also be a relief to have told the worst and discover that your supervisor seems relatively unmoved by the revelation.

Sometimes supervisees seem bent on concealing material relating to what they said in the session; if this appears to be happening, it needs to be addressed. It is easier for supervisees to be honest if their accounts of interventions they regret making are met with a sympathetic and measured interest rather than outright condemnation. But the supervisor needs to hang on to their own idea of what is good practice even if the supervisee is easily wounded, and good practice in supervision does involve honesty and frankness on both sides as well as tact. We need to be able to create an atmosphere where there can be a mutual exploration of issues of concern, as free as possible from the influence of the critical, omnipotent superego which, as we have seen in Chapter 3, can easily enter into supervision.

The act of writing up a process recording can also allow the supervisee to manage their anxiety until it is time for supervision. This might be particularly important when the session has been disturbing, when writing the notes can have a containing function:

Anna had had a difficult session with a new student client, who had also seen several of her colleagues in the college in which she worked, idealising and denigrating them all in turn. Realising that the client was attempting to divide and rule in terms of his interactions with other professionals, Anna had stood up to the client; she had told him she would not write a report he was asking for (this was not in fact either necessary or appropriate, and she told him this). The client had become very angry, shouting, accusing her of incompetence, unhelpfulness and saying he would complain to the Dean, and so on, and then walked out. Anna had felt completely flattened by the client, and as she said later, quite guilty, anxious and paranoid.

Anna didn't normally write up detailed notes of all sessions (she had a heavy caseload) but took particular care in this case, since she was so upset by it, as well as concerned for the client. In the process she paid attention to what she had said, and was able to see that she had actually handled the session quite well, and done as much as she possibly could. By the time she got to supervision a day or two later, she was feeling much calmer. Even if the client did complain, she felt she would be able to give a good account of the encounter. She had been able to stand back and look at the encounter from a different perspective.

Difficulties in writing process notes

Many supervisees do not find this task easy at first; we can probably all recall instances in our own training when writing up the session seemed an imposition, a burdensome activity and even at times an impossible one, because we could not remember what had happened in any detail. But supervisees in training need to be asked to persist with it, as once they are able to do this it is an invaluable aid to further thinking about the clients and their dilemmas. And continuous practice at writing notes helps to develop the capacity to remember and make sense of the session. If workable notes are not forthcoming, the supervisor needs to explore what is the area of difficulty; a number of possibilities come to mind. Some might be related primarily to the way the supervisee is seeing the world, perhaps to anxieties to do with starting work:

In the example of John, the 'difficult' supervisee from Chapter 3, one of the problems that his supervisor reported was difficulty in bringing notes. In this case, it seemed as if an acute anxiety about beginning the work was masked initially by a rebellious, rivalrous attitude which was particularly in evidence towards his (male) supervisor. Not being able to bring notes might be one aspect of a generally difficult supervisory relationship, in which Robert too played his part, as he was very ready to acknowledge. Robert, talking of the situation, said, 'to begin with I thought he was just being awkward – and there was an element of his thinking that he was entitled to special treatment, because he was so busy outside the placement – no time to write up sessions in any detail. But as time went on I realised that it was more than that. It was partly that he really couldn't bear for me to scrutinise his work, but underneath that I think he really had not got the capacity, at that point in his development, to make enough sense of the session to remember it. It was his anxiety that disabled him, particularly in the early stages – later on things became easier.'

In addition to the potential disabling effects of the supervisee's anxieties, the clients being worked with may well have a level of disturbance which 'gets into' the account of the session, via projective identification and the supervisee's countertransference, and this possibility always has to be considered when a supervisee finds notes about a particular client or patient difficult to write. It usually happens that as the supervisee becomes more accustomed to supervision, the work context and working with the client, it becomes more possible to give an account of the session – and the way in which it is presented might well give a clue to the nature of the client's difficulties. I would suggest that this is because the trainee has begun to empathise with or understand the patient, often at an unconscious level. The inner world of the patient becomes more meaningful and this makes it possible to remember more of what happens in the session. Sometimes this seems to be related to a link than has been made with a theory or part of a theory, an example of the containing function of theory in allowing different ways of looking at the material. Of course it is also to do with a developing relationship between the supervisor and the supervisee.

When the supervisee persistently presents notes that give a chaotic impression, and this is a general feature of their work, the supervisor should consider the possibility that the supervisee is in trouble, possibly because the training on which they are embarked has stirred up some very deep-rooted anxieties which are threatening their ability to function. Or there may be difficulties or crises in other areas of the supervisee's life. In this case it is usually obvious in other ways that something is wrong and needs to be addressed. Often supervisees will let us know of such situations.

At the other extreme, able and conscientious supervisees may bring very long and coherent accounts of their sessions, far too much to be considered within the time. If they are writing up a patient for a case study then this will be useful, but sometimes there can be a sense of disappointment at not being able to consider it all. I think this tendency may also reflect the need we all have at times, to check that we are on the right lines. Sometimes bringing very long notes has a defensive quality, in that going through them in any detail may preclude the supervisor making much sense of it, in terms of the content, and does not allow much time for free association. The dynamics of this situation may need to be thought about, but the supervisor also needs to take responsibility for structuring the supervision session so that there is enough time to make it possible to reflect together on the account of the session. Otherwise you may find yourself intervening in less helpful ways. I find that I am more likely to interrupt the supervisee or get somewhat didactic if I think that the reported session will be an extra long account or there will be no room for my input.

The material from the process recording stimulates a freer exploration of feelings and thoughts as well as allowing for a more detailed consideration of the session when we reflect what has gone on.

Reporting on sessions – more experienced therapists

When therapists have completed their training they require something different from supervision. A more collegiate atmosphere is appropriate, which does not imply that supervision should be any less challenging – in fact I find that more experienced supervisees can often want to be challenged more. They are likely to have more of a sense of their own strengths, and a debate about aspects of the case does not touch on their own sense of self-worth as much as for those at the beginning of their careers. And very often supervisees who are qualified will be presenting work from a heavy caseload; they are less likely to be in a position to focus exclusively on one patient on an ongoing basis. I do not ask such supervisees to bring full process notes, although it is useful as I have found in my own supervision to write up more fully the parts of the sessions that seem significant.

Often, more experienced supervisees are able to give a vivid account of the session without necessarily needing to go into such detail over the content; they are more likely to be focussing on the relationship between them and the client rather than simply giving an account of what was said. However the above example of Anna and the angry client draws attention to the usefulness of writing up really difficult sessions in more detail, in terms of containing anxiety.

Thoughts and feelings about the session – the supervisee's reaction to the client

Often the supervisee will mention thoughts or feelings that they had in the session or just after it; the supervisor needs to indicate from the start that such material is helpful to understanding the events of the sessions at a deeper level. Part of the purpose of this is to alert the supervisee to the fact that they should not take the client's point of view at face value. In addition, counsellors and therapists beginning training are apt to undervalue their countertransference, having an idea that analytic neutrality means suppressing their own reactions.

And sometimes they can feel that their own views result from their own psychopathology or past history and are therefore something to be ashamed of, or at least ignored. Nevertheless, as experienced practitioners know, thoughts and ideas that seem at variance with the apparent theme of the session can be a way of revealing something that has not to date been thought about consciously. The following example illustrates something of this.

> *Alice was a trainee beginning work with a male patient. The material she brought to supervision had a rather flat quality and at times the supervisor found herself almost drifting off as the account unfolded. It was not helped by the fact that this was a very silent patient so the actual content in terms of what was said was sparse, and limited to rather prosaic descriptions of his daily life. The supervisor thought and said that the patient needed to be confronted about the apparent censorship he was operating in what he brought to the sessions, and that Alice generally needed to challenge the patient more. She realised that Alice was inexperienced, but wondered also whether there was an excessive concern about the reaction she would get from the patient.*
>
> *Certainly it seemed that there were thoughts and feelings that weren't being expressed by either the patient or the therapist, and she eventually asked Alice whether she was frightened of the patient. This revealed a much richer and, to Alice, disturbing, series of fantasies and thoughts. Alice said what she found disconcerting was the way her mind kept wandering; she found it difficult to concentrate particularly in the silences.*
>
> *The supervisor asked whether there was anything that came to mind in these silences. Alice talked of disconcertingly violent images; when asked to elaborate she talked of an idea of a heart transplant. a road accident. She went on, 'I don't know where these ideas come from – it's rather shocking, why would I be thinking like this? ... some of it might be me, (she made a reference to an earlier experience) ... do you mean that they (ideas) might be related to the patient? I hadn't thought of that.'*
>
> *After a pause she said, 'I thought I actually quite liked him ... but now I'm not sure ... perhaps there is a ruthless quality to him .... that I hadn't thought about before.'*

By listening to and exploring these ideas, the supervisor encouraged Alice to take her own experience seriously, as a countertransference reaction. She established that these were not just random thoughts but associated particularly with the sessions with this patient. Although they couldn't be sure of their meaning, they were able to speculate that the patient's presentation might be a way of concealing, even from himself, some very violent thoughts. (There are other explanations; the fantasies might also say something, for example, about his experience of the therapy as violently intrusive.)

Alice put these ideas to the back of her mind (and was privately sceptical) but a few weeks later the patient came and reported that he had got into a fight with a neighbour 'over a sort of boundary dispute'; he was lucky the man was not taking him to court as he'd punched him a couple of times, and hadn't wanted to stop. He then quickly moved to another subject. At this point Alice was able to use her previous experience and her discussion in supervision. She pursued the issue of violence with the patient, in terms of realistic concerns about the effect of this on his daily life, and his apparent refusal to take the issue seriously, and so demonstrated that she was robust enough to work on these issues. We could also hypothesise that Alice's increased awareness of a possible issue about violence, following the supervision, communicated itself to the patient at an unconscious level and allowed him to broach the subject.

This example highlights the need for supervisors to be curious about apparently random thoughts and associations that might have a bearing on the dynamics of the session. Of course such thoughts also need to be seen in the context of other material that is being presented, or experienced. In this case we can hypothesise that something was being conveyed by the patient via projective identification that could not initially be processed by the supervisee; the supervisor picked it up because of her own sense of unease.

Reflecting on what has gone on

In the above example we can see that the supervisor was able to take a step back and ask a question which related to a sense that there was something missing about the account given by the supervisee that hadn't been expressed in words. This of course is one of the crucial characteristics of supervision, that the supervisor can have an overview because of being one removed from the encounter with the patient or client.

This overview can take account of evidence from three main sources – the account, written or otherwise, that the supervisee brings to the session, the thoughts and feelings that the supervisee has about the session and the supervisor's own thoughts and reactions about what has transpired. But as we have seen in Chapter 1, the supervisor is also looking at the material in the light of their own thoughts about supervision priorities at this point in time – monitoring as opposed to educative for example – and the way in which the material is taken up may reflect the predominance of one or other of these. The question of more serious concerns – for example risks to the client/patient, or to the therapist – is considered more specifically in Chapter 9.

When supervision is going well, there is space to think about the material and play with it, with both people producing ideas and associations that allow for the development of a fuller understanding of the patient. There can be a sense of connection and creativity in the thinking that goes on; the sense of jointly discovering something new is one of the pleasures of supervision. This process is always informed by our own internalised theories, which are there in the background to shape our thinking. I find when I am supervising that there are a number of preliminary ways of looking at the material that I allow to come to mind; these may seem obvious in theory but in practice can easily be overlooked.

As with the case of Alice and the violent patient, set out above, we need to listen for the gaps in the narrative, for what is **not** being said or recorded in the account of the session. In that case there was a sense of flatness or deadness in the account, or expressed by the supervisee, which concealed stronger feelings.

We need to watch out for things that do not seem to make sense or are incongruous. There might be a discrepancy between the manifest content of the session and the mood or feelings related to the encounter, as experienced by either the supervisee or the supervisor. I find that sometimes I may be listening to an account of a session and think that what is being said in the way of interventions is very appropriate. But then I will realise with a jolt that it is all being said in a very calm or disengaged way, and I realise that for some reason the supervisee is concerned not to rock the boat. The example of Alice and the violent patient, above, is a dramatic version of this phenomenon, but there may be other reasons why the supervisee thinks that it is best to keep things peaceful, and these may need to be explored before any real change can take place in the way the supervisee relates to the patient or client.

Or the supervisee may accept too readily what is said in the sessions, when this may be contradicted by the way counselling is used, as the following example shows:

Angela, a trainee counsellor, was working with a very depressed client who was constantly 15 minutes late for her sessions, which were at 10 AM. Angela accepted the client's explanation that she was too depressed to get up in time for her session. But she felt on the whole things were going well; she had also accepted the client's assurances that she was really very happy with the counselling and was finding it very useful.

Although the supervisor knew that depression often made people feel worse in the mornings, she was sceptical about the client's explanation in this case, and urged Angela to keep an open mind and explore the issues further with the client. A little while later, Angela had an afternoon vacancy and decided that she would change the session time to later in the day. For a week or so the client was on time. She then reverted to her former pattern of being 15 minutes late for every session.

When they discussed this matter in supervision, the supervisor realised that Angela was at an early stage in terms of being able to apply the psychodynamic understanding that she was learning on her course. She had understood in theory that actions had a meaning which might contradict what was actually said in the sessions, but at this point she could not see how this might be demonstrated in practice. The client's continuing lateness brought home to her very powerfully that there must be some other explanation, which she thought about in supervision. This allowed her to question the rather prosaic version of events that she had accepted up to then, as well as her need to try to make things easier for the client. But until she had really understood this dynamic she was unable to say anything to the client.

Transference and countertransference: focussing on identifications

Putting together the information on what happened in the session together with the ideas and feelings that emerge on reflection allows the supervisor and supervisee to think together about the overall nature of the transference/countertransference, which in turn provides information about the internal objects of the patient or client (see also Chapter 4). Every supervisor will have developed their own perspectives on this, based on the way in which they have integrated the theory they have been taught with their own experience and practice. These perspectives provide a basis for a more disciplined focus on the session.

In thinking about this, I have found Heinrich Racker's (1968) work on transference and countertransference very useful.

He distinguishes between concordant countertransference, which is based on the therapist's identification with the patient, and complementary countertransference, where the therapist seems to be identified with one or more of the patient's internal objects. He sees the first type of identification, the concordant countertransference, as resulting from the therapist's attempt to understand the patient by empathising with them. This happens, mainly at an unconscious level, when we listen to patients and try to use our own experiences to find a point of contact or understanding. This is the positive side of this type of countertransference as described by Racker.

However, often counsellors at the beginning of their training are apt to identify too closely with their clients or patients, resulting sometimes in a tendency to turn a blind eye to their negative or destructive side. This may be the case with Angela above – in her efforts to understand the client and her inability to get to the sessions on time, she finds herself ignoring the fact that the client is destroying a part of what is available to her in terms of the counselling. Where there is this type of identification, the verbatim reports presented in supervision tend to be rather concrete, with an underlying assumption that everything the client says is literally true. When challenged about this supervisees may feel that the veracity of the client is being questioned, because they have not yet been able to establish for themselves that clients are talking about their internal objects and not necessarily about the 'real life' parental or other figure.

Part of the work of supervision at this point is to keep in mind the stage the supervisee is at, in terms of understanding. It may help to point out that there are different versions of the truth, and that we are not doubting the strength of the client's feelings or their belief on their own story. We learn through experience that people's ideas about their own history are not fixed for all time, and the way in which these ideas change over time, even in one session, helps us to build up an idea of the concept of internal objects and what this means in practice. The supervisor can help this understanding to develop by standing back from the material being presented and giving their understanding of the narrative.

Racker sees the second type of countertransference as developing when the therapist cannot identify with the patient for various reasons and finds themselves taking up a particular (negative) stance in relation to the patient. He considers that the two types of countertransference are effectively present in most therapeutic encounters, as the dynamics of the work unfold. Complementary countertransference is often the result of some anxiety which the therapist is feeling in response to a perceived threat from the patient. The example Racker gives is that of a patient threatening suicide, where the therapist may initially feel annoyed as well as concerned. But guilt about these feelings may result in a renewed attempt to identify with the patient in a more empathetic way (op. cit., p. 136) as well as see the destructive side.

In the example of Mary and the depressed student that I described in Chapter 3, it seems that initially Mary was unable to empathize with the student on a conscious level. (This seems to be an example of the complementary countertransference that Racker is writing about.) However later events showed that she had seen similarities between her experience and that of the student, but that these has been painful to think about and so she had pushed them away. Initially this had given her work and her account of the sessions a lifeless quality, but matters came to a head when she found herself getting angry with him. This was a painful experience for them both but resulted in a much more empathetic approach to the student's difficulties.

As supervisors we need to be alert to the unconscious dynamics operating in the sessions with clients, but we also need to pay attention to our own position in the triangle; otherwise we are liable to act according to our own identifications. In the above example, the supervisor might have been tempted to be impatient with the supervisee, because of her own more sympathetic identification with the student client. We need to use our emotional experience to help the supervisee understand what is going on in the work with the client.

Other combinations of concordant and complementary countertransference are also very common in supervision. For example, we may have to think about our own sustained close identification with the supervisee. While this may be seen as part of a good working alliance, it sometimes means that the patient's point of view is not being considered enough, and the supervisee is not being sufficiently challenged. When supervision seems to be going well, we still have to keep in mind the possibility that difficult issues are being collusively avoided.

A further variation is one where the supervisee and their client or patient are closely identified, and the supervisor feels excluded. Sometimes this comes about through a defensiveness on the part of the supervisee, but it may also be related to the dynamics of the case.

This can be related to 'real life' differences between supervisor and supervisee.

> Caroline, a counsellor working at a young people's counselling service, was working with Katrina, a young woman who had been sexually and physically abused as a child by her father. Although her own experience had not been so traumatic, Caroline was able to identify with Katrina's issues in what seemed initially a very helpful way. It was clear to her supervisor, a man, that a good working alliance had been forged and that for Katrina, being able to talk about her experience had been a great relief.
>
> As time went on the supervisor realised he was hearing less and less about the content of the sessions. When he asked questions about the work, he felt as if he was intruding. When this was explored Caroline admitted that she felt inhibited about exposing her client in supervision. She had over identified with the client's issues to the point where a different (male) perspective was seen as uncomfortable, even threatening to the relationship they had developed.

Projective identification and pressures towards enactments

An aspect of the countertransference that helps us to understand what is going on is the **strength** of the feelings that the session engenders, a point made by Thomas Ogden (1982) among others, writing about projective identification. He defines projective identification as 'the aspect of transference that involves the therapist in an interpersonal actualisation (an actual enactment between patient and therapist) of a segment of the patient's internal object world' (p. 77). When very strong feelings are being engendered in a session it is very difficult to maintain a reflective stance. (I should make it clear that I am thinking mainly about verbal enactments here rather than more serious boundary violations.)

This point is also made by Betty Joseph (e.g., in 'On understanding and not understanding' (1982)). She writes about invasive projective identification on the part of patients who are not interested in understanding, but in the course of trying to **be** understood project strong feelings and sensations into the analyst, who may have great difficulty in not acting out in one way or another (p. 149). John Steiner (2006), developing this theme, sees enactments as a breach of the frame or setting and considers that 'they must be tolerated as part of the analyst's ordinary fallibility, but monitored as a check on our self understanding and our contact with reality' (p. 315). He points out that verbal enactments are often disguised as interpretations (op. cit., p. 317).

In supervision we have to begin by helping our supervisees to recognise enactments – as Steiner points out, they cannot be used to understand the patient unless they are recognised. Sometimes the supervisee will be only too aware of having in some way stepped out of role, and often this will be related to unconscious communications from the client/patient. Very often there is a more subtle attack on the boundaries. Going over the process recording and thinking about the nature of the interventions that are made can allow us to see when the supervisee has been pressured into taking up a particular role (critical authority figure, friend, that of trying to bring the client to life and so on) or when there may be a tendency to intellectualise, educate or develop an over cognitive approach. Jane Milton (2001) writes of the difficulty in maintaining an analytic stance, which in so many ways runs counter to normal ways of relating to people, and of the pressure the patient puts on the analyst to move towards a more cognitive or behavioural stance, with interpretations taking the form of disguised practical suggestions.

Less benignly, an interpretation may be a form of retaliation from a despairing therapist, as the following example illustrates:

> Anita brought to supervision a patient she was seeing in private practice. He was proving more difficult – and anxiety provoking – to work with than she had envisaged, being very depressed and at times expressing thoughts about self harm, seeming very out of contact. Sessions tended to turn in to a sort of rant about his difficult relationships with Anita occasionally making a comment – the supervisor noted that she veered between a somewhat disempowered silence punctuated by the occasional rather sharp comment. It felt as if there was an argument waiting to happen. Eventually Anita, after a number of deadening rebuffs, told how she had raised her voice and (almost) shouted 'it seems as if you're giving me an experience at this very moment of how your relationships get so tangled up'.
>
> Silence had fallen; the patient had eventually said, 'I don't know what you mean; . . . now you've totally confused me . . .'. He had relapsed into silence for the rest of the session.
>
> A few days later, he had left a message on Anita's answer phone saying he'd decided not to come to therapy any more.

Supervisors might have various reactions to Anita's account. But we can understand what was going on in terms of her being at the receiving end of a great deal of projective identification, which she initially attempted to bear silently. In her head, she made the link between his difficulties and the way he was behaving in the session with her, but her first attempts to intervene were rebuffed. In her efforts to get through to him, she found herself getting more intense. However the way in which she formulated her intervention and the tone in which she said it turned out to be counterproductive, since her underlying aim was to rid herself of the difficult feelings he had pushed into her.

In supervision, Anita said that she hadn't realised how affected she was by the extent of her patient's hostility; she had felt quite unable to empathise with what was undoubtedly a very depressed and despairing patient. She also felt guilty abut having taken him on in the first place. She didn't think she could work with this man at this point in her career, and certainly not in her own consulting room. This realisation had added to her sense of persecution in the session and resulted eventually in this vengeful comment. As it turned out, the patient did have other ways of getting help, which may have been more suitable.

We need to try to identify and think about verbal enactments in supervision, since their extent and nature provides a clue to what is going on with the patient. Patients who have less serious issues do not put the same pressure on the therapist to get involved in a mutual enactment of transference and countertransference issues; the therapist will generally be more able to empathise imaginatively with the patient. They may also be more able to maintain a separateness from the patient and to challenge them.

Helping the supervisee think about the course of further work

In the preceding sections we have thought about how to understand what has transpired in the session, in its broadest sense, focussing particularly on transference and countertransference issues. We can use this knowledge to make an assessment of the areas of the work that need further thought on the part of the supervisee. What we decide to highlight will relate to the supervisee's qualities and characteristics as well as those of the patient.

In this context I have found David Tuckett's (2005) paper 'Does anything go?' very useful. In this paper he suggests that, despite differences in theoretical formulations, there are common aspects of working within the analytic tradition which can be used to think about the presented session. Although he is concerned with assessment in a more formal sense, in terms of assessing candidates' progress in training, I think his suggestions have a wider relevance for anyone supervising within the psychodynamic tradition. He is concerned with general indicators about progress and level of working which are not dependent on those making the assessment agreeing on the details of the theory underpinning the work. These indicators relate to the use of the setting, developing a conceptual frame, and thinking about interventions, all aspects which those supervising less experienced practitioners need to keep in mind. I am focusing briefly here on the questions of boundaries and the supervisee's interventions.

We have already seen that creating a bounded setting is at the heart of the psychodynamic approach, and when the material presented shows a lack of attention to boundaries the supervisor will need to address this issue as a priority. Without a bounded approach to the work the supervisee will be unable to provide a containing setting where difficult issues can be explored (Chapter 2).

It is important for supervisors to keep in mind the effects of absences, time changes and breaks on the course of the therapeutic work, and suggest ways of addressing these. This is particularly true for inexperienced therapists who may not have had enough of their own therapy to be aware of the impact of breaks. (The example of Angela, who altered the time of her client's appointment, is a case in point.) In this context, they may need help in terms of what they might say to their patients; discussion of ways of addressing issues is sometimes demanded and may be helpful. Once supervisees can think about their experience of what is happening they are usually able to find their own words, and they do need to find their own voice.

As supervisors, we expect to find that relatively inexperienced therapists need help with these issues. Attention to boundaries is not something to take for granted in more experienced workers, however. On the whole, they will be aware of the importance of the setting and will bring up their concerns when they find themselves being drawn into these forms of enactments. But sometimes we can be alarmed by seemingly casual references to practices that could potentially make the patient feel unsafe and confused; it is usually the lack of awareness or thought that is disconcerting.

Developing a conceptual framework relating to the patient's difficulties is something that may take time, as we know from our own work as therapists. In the course of hearing about the session we have probably developed some preliminary ideas, however tentative and provisional. We need, when hearing abut a first session, to think with the supervisee about the seriousness of the concerns being brought to the sessions, whether the material suggests neurotic difficulties or something more serious.

Suggestions for interventions need to take account of what we have learned about the patient, the supervisee's relationship with the patient and their level of experience and understanding. One important factor, particularly for those beginning therapeutic work, is the extent to which the supervisee's interpretations show that they are emotionally in touch with the patient, and their current state of mind. We have seen that an advantage of a detailed process recording is that we may be able to show the supervisee instances where something that has been said clearly increases rapport in the session – or the reverse – and this helps the supervisee think about work in the future.

> A new supervisee, Joe, brought an account of his work with Miss L, a woman who had come to counselling after being dismissed from her job. In the first few sessions Miss L went over and over the circumstances of this event and her subsequent appeal to her employers. Joe found it difficult to make sense of the story, and found himself asking questions and on one occasion pointing out a discrepancy in her account. He realised this was a mistake when he saw what he'd written about the session – her reply, although not overtly angry, was to do with the intrusive and critical nature of her employers. But the supervisor was able to point out how he had recovered the situation a few minutes later, when he had said something that showed himself to be more in touch with her frustration and depression – he had commented that perhaps she felt that no one, including him, could understand how difficult her situation was. This had elicited a much more reflective response. Seeing the impact of what he said allowed Joe to think more analytically about his work and the nature of his interaction with the client.

Supervisees who are too soothing or too abrasive need to be encouraged to think about this, as do those with a tendency to cram too much into a single intervention, or present something in a confused way. Sometimes interventions reflect an anxiety on the part of the supervisee, or a desire to break a silence, or move away from painful issues. We also need to see whether the supervisee is able to note and comment on the patient's response to the intervention.

Just as the supervisee has to think about what to say to the patient, so we have to think about how we intervene in supervision; we might have to think about our own habitual responses or whether we are getting caught up in some form of enactment, possibly related to some sort of parallel process.

Throughout this chapter I have emphasised the importance of helping the supervisee to reflect on the interaction in the session. If the supervisee can maintain a position as a participant observer, for most of the time, their interventions or interpretations are likely to be sensitive and in tune with the state of mind of the patient.

Finally, I think it is important to accept how difficult it can be, for many reasons, to make an effective interpretation; this is not just about levels of experience but also our concerns – or fantasies – about the vulnerability of the patient. Some of these concerns are related to the powerful effect of the projective identification to which the therapist is subject; we have seen this in some of the examples given in this chapter. Robert Caper in his book *A Mind of One's Own* (1999) thinks in some detail about inhibitions in making interpretations. We can be pulled into a state of mind where the idea of making an interpretation that will make a difference to the patient, and thus make them aware of their separateness gives rise to a sense of danger in the therapist. As experienced therapists we know this to be true; part of the task of supervision is to help our supervisees think about this difficulty. We also have to keep in mind that there are many circumstances where interpretations are not appropriate, perhaps because of the literal way in which they might be received.

Summary and conclusions

This chapter has considered in more detail what might happen in a supervision session and the tasks that the supervisor has to keep in mind. The process of supervision is illustrated by different examples and we consider how our understanding of relevant theory might contribute to its practice. In the course of finding out what went on in the session with the patient or client, we think about aspects of the countertransference engendered by the session and how this deepens our understanding of the patient's concerns. We become aware of the dynamics that might originate with the patient, and in their relationship with the supervisee. When it comes to thinking with the supervisee on ways of conveying what we have found out to the patient, supervisees may initially need help in formulating their interventions; in this context, the inherent difficulties of working psychodynamically at any level need to be kept in mind.

Some concluding points are set out below:

- Supervision involves a drawing on a number of sources of information – the accounts of what was said and experienced, together with a more considered view of the dynamics at a deeper level. We have to find a balance between the value we give to these different aspects, keeping enough distance to see what is missing from the account. The way in which we make suggestions to the supervisee, in terms of the course of future work, will depend very much on idiosyncratic aspects of the supervisory relationship, as well as on characteristics of the supervisee and aspects of their experience. There is a balance between arriving at a shared understanding and making explicit suggestions.

- When supervisees present instances of interactions where they are conscious of some kind of misunderstanding or enactment, for example, showing a lack in empathy, it is usually more productive to help them think about the causes of these dynamics than to be critical. Under these circumstances, the supervisee is often feeling guilty in any case. (It is much more worrying when one gets a glimpse of something having happened without an awareness of anything being wrong.)

- Nevertheless, supervision always involves assessment, even if not in a formal sense – it is part of the role. If we are to be helpful to our supervisees we have to think about their contributions to the therapeutic process and be prepared to make it clear when their habitual ways of working – those relating to boundaries and the setting, as well as the way in which they intervene in sessions – need to be reconsidered.

SUPERVISING GROUPS

Introduction

This chapter considers aspects of the dynamics involved in group supervision, which bring a further level of complexity to the process. In many settings it is the form of supervision most commonly on offer, partly for reasons of economy. Counselling trainings and community counselling services often offer group supervision, as do many NHS settings. There are many practical advantages: trainees have the opportunity to learn from other possibly more experienced counsellors and therapists as well as the supervisor; and different professional groups can learn something of each others' work. Supervisees realise that they are not alone in finding particular situations difficult.

If a group is running well, there can be a supportive atmosphere which encourages disclosure and contributes to the learning of all the participants. The differing experiences of members of the group mean that a greater variety of reactions – hypotheses, associations and suggestions – are available for thinking about the clients. Actual differences in the membership – whether related to ethnic origin, gender, age or other characteristics – can be a source of learning. And a creative use of parallel processes operating in the group can provide additional information on the client/supervisee relationship. Supervising in groups is often enjoyable for the supervisor.

But things do not always go so well. Supervisees can feel exposed, and while it can be more difficult to address points of conflict or criticism in a group, the impact of what is said often seems amplified by the fact that others are hearing it too. We can probably all remember occasions when we dreaded presenting in seminar or supervision groups. We can feel that our patient – as well as our sense of our self as a competent practitioner – has got lost in the welter of other opinions and ideas. There is usually less time to consider each patient, and pressure on time contributes to competition for space within the group. In any group there is an inevitable and innate competitiveness (all the more powerful for being denied at times) and this can result in the group getting sidetracked into destructive ways of dealing with this.

Rivalry can also be exacerbated if a supervision group has a membership drawn from various professional backgrounds, as happens in many organisations. Very often in this case the intention is that in addition to receiving supervision the different groups shall come to understand the particular constraints and challenges of their role, and that of others, within the organisation. However, sharing information and concern can engender rivalrous feelings, as the following vignette demonstrates:

A supervisee working in a primary care setting reported how uncomfortable she could feel in group supervision when the practice nurses spoke about their work. They talked of the large numbers of patients they had to see within a relatively short time scale, and it was clear they envied the counsellors with their 50-minute appointment slots, sometimes using phases such as 'of course, we also do counselling in our work'. But the counsellor realised that she too could feel quite envious – the nurses seemed to have more satisfied customers and were able to be helpful in a more immediate, practical way that gave them a sense of having been useful. She sometimes felt that her patients left her with all the negative feelings about the services the practice was providing.

Part of the task of the group supervisor in this situation might be to think about the rivalry within the group and how it might affect the way members carry out their tasks within the organisation. But the supervisor has also to be able to think of their own role and the extent to which it is appropriate to interpret these dynamics, leaning towards providing consultation to the group rather than supervision of the work with patients. It is very easy to get sidetracked and pulled out of role. The particular demands of working within an organisational setting will be considered in the next chapter.

Supervising in groups therefore poses challenges which may relate to the context in which the group takes place as well as their inherent characteristics. I would suggest that ideally, counsellors in training benefit from a period of individual supervision, but this is not always an option within an institution. We need to find constructive ways of understanding and using group supervision, and the chapter concludes with some practical suggestions.

First, however, it is useful to elaborate on the potential dynamics of groups, the pitfalls and the opportunities. We have probably all been in supervision groups where the group as a group has been effectively ignored and what took place was a series of individual supervisions, with the other group members keeping quiet when it was not their turn. But this approach means that an important source of information – the group's reactions to what is being presented, including the variety of countertransference reactions – is lost. How can we take account of the extra dimensions and possibilities relating to the group dynamics while still keeping in mind the clients and their relationship with the supervisees?

For psychotherapists and counsellors working primarily with individuals, thinking about and working with groups may involve a radical shift in perspective. Such a shift may not be comfortable; we may have chosen to work on a one-to-one basis precisely because we value the potential intimacy of such work, and find the strength of feelings engendered in a group – particularly those relating to competition and rivalry – more difficult to manage.

In addition, groups can engender a deeper level of anxiety to do with fears of losing our own sense of identity, as well as a sense that other people may become a different version of themselves when they are in a group. The idea of the group having so much influence over its individual members can be disconcerting for those who are not used to thinking and working in groups. It involves having to reconsider a more familiar perspective, based on the triangular constellation of the patient, supervisee and supervisor.

While many of the dynamics relating to individual supervision, including the kind of competitiveness which relates to our unresolved Oedipal issues, will also apply when supervising in groups, we need to accept that groups have their own culture and momentum, where to a certain extent individuals' usual ways of relating are subordinated to the influence of the group, and the context in which it is situated.

Theories about groups

Freud (1921), considering the nature of the group's influence on the individual, hypothesised that the group members were bound together emotionally by the energy (libido) relating to instinctual impulses, which became directed to a common aim. These emotional ties were the result of identification on the part of group members, with each other and with the leader of the group who represented the ego ideal.

Since the time Freud was writing, a large body of theory relating to group processes and group therapy has been generated. (See, e.g., Farhad Dalal (1998) *Taking the Group Seriously* which gives a very comprehensive review of the various strands of influence on current group analytic theory.) Most supervisors working one-to-one will not have had a group analytic training, but there are other conceptualisations which are useful for exploring the dynamics. Some of these spring from a psychoanalytic tradition, but others such as systems theory and group relations can also be helpful.

There is not the space in this context to do justice to these ideas, or to group theory generally, but I begin by setting out Bion's ideas on groups which, while developed in a different context, have a great deal to contribute to thinking about the potential dynamics that develop in supervision groups. As in individual supervision, being able to have a framework for thinking about what is going on helps to ensure that the group, including the supervisor, is not unduly distracted from the task of supervision by the various ways in which different types of anxiety are acted out. Bion's ideas will also be useful for thinking about supervising those working in institutions, which is the subject of the next chapter.

Bion's contribution to thinking about groups

Bion's theories, set out in *Experiences in Groups* (1961), have been very influential in thinking about group behaviour, particularly in a group relations context but also in other situations. Many of his ideas were based on small groups which he conducted at the Tavistock Clinic in the late 1940s but he also drew on his experience of groups within institutions, gained during the Second World War in the course of working as an army officer and as a medical officer in a rehabilitation unit. Although his ideas were developed in the context of somewhat larger groups than most supervision groups, they are invaluable in highlighting some of the ways in which a group's anxiety can be expressed.

The work group

Bion distinguished two main ways for a group to function. One of these is the work group. As he wrote (op. cit., p. 143):

Every group, however casual, meets to 'do' something; in this activity, according to the capacities of the individuals, they cooperate. This cooperation is voluntary and depends on some degree of sophisticated skill in the individual...participation in this activity is possible only to individuals with years of training and a capacity for experience that has permitted them to develop mentally. Since this activity is geared to a task, it is related to reality, its methods are rational, and therefore, in however embryonic form, scientific. Its characteristics are similar to those attributed by Freud (1911) to the ego. This facet of mental activity in a group I have called the work group.

The work group, then, is what we might hope of a supervision group – cooperative, because based on a common purpose, thoughtful, task oriented, reality based and therefore capable of learning from experience.

Basic assumption functioning

However, Bion found that there was another side to group functioning; he found that membership of a group activated a particular type of (largely unconscious) anxiety. He considered this level of anxiety to be associated with a regression to what Klein has described as the paranoid-schizoid position, where destructive forces within the individual are projected into the object and then experienced as a threat from the outside. (For a clear description of this way of functioning as it relates to individuals, see, e.g., Steiner (1992).) Group members in this state of mind will have a tendency to view others and events in a polarised way – they may be idealised or denigrated, quite unrealistically. In addition intolerable feelings of anxiety will be got rid of by projective identification, feelings which will then be experienced very powerfully by the other members of the group, including the person responsible for running the group. When this happens, as Bion writes, there is a sense of 'being manipulated so as to be playing a part, no matter how difficult to recognise, in someone else's phantasy' (op. cit., p. 149). But he adds that a temporary loss of insight into what is going on may make it difficult to recognise this situation.

There are therefore powerful emotional drives operating at a largely unconscious level which constantly threaten to undermine the activities of the work group, since energy is deflected from the 'real' task of the group into defending against anxiety. Bion considered that these took the form of shared phantasies which he termed Basic Assumptions, meaning that they are unconscious assumptions about the purpose of the group, which are at variance with the stated task. Bion's basic assumptions are those of dependency, pairing and fight or flight, and any group can demonstrate one or all three in sequence when they get together.

Dependency (baD)

In groups where learning is part of the task, baD is a very likely development. It involves an assumption on the part of the group that they are meeting to receive something more than understanding or insight – perhaps nourishment, or protection – in a very literal way. Of course when we come to a supervision group we have the right to expect that the supervisor will facilitate our learning or teach us in more direct ways, but a group in baD mode will tend to act as though this should happen by magic, without any effort on their part. There is a sense of a very passive state of mind, as though knowledge can just be painlessly passed from one mind to another. This state of mind may well appear as a reaction to events that the group has not been able to digest; the following example shows a group apparently immobilised:

Kathy, who was new to group supervision, had taken over a supervision group of six trainee counsellors in a counselling service following the sudden retirement through ill health of the previous supervisor, a very experienced and popular figure. It seemed as though their worries about the nature of this departure and the loss of their supervisor had affected them all in a similar way, although Kathy did not make this connection to begin with.

In the group, material would be presented about sessions with their clients which suggested that the participants were stuck in a painful, depressed way of relating. Absences and missed sessions were reported on in tones of resignation, and the group as a whole, although showing sympathy to whoever was presenting, seemed very unwilling to engage with each other in a lively way. There seemed little differentiation between the clients being presented. A pattern developed of individual presentations being followed by a sense of expectation, giving way to a stuck, sullen silence; it was clear that the group thought that Kathy was the one who should provide the answers.

Kathy found herself being very active in this group, making rather concrete suggestions for interventions and experiencing a tendency to want to liven things up, by being rather more challenging than usual. This did not have the desired effect, and then she too would feel despair and exasperation. The whole process was excruciating; she began to dread the afternoons when the group met.

Kathy thought about the situation; she realised that the group was acting in Dependency mode, where the members had regressed to a point where they felt deskilled and powerless as well as hopeless. To begin with, Kathy had not thought about the nature of the underlying anxiety except in terms of a **change** in supervisor – she had initially tried to get their reactions to this. She thought perhaps the other supervisor had encouraged a more dependent attitude and she found herself feeling quite angry with him. Then she realised that anger and aggression seemed to be being experienced by her, for various reasons, but were strikingly absent in the overt behaviour of other members of the group. This made her realise that there were some powerful projective processes going on, and she came to the conclusion that the group had not been able to process their anger and upset about the loss of their previous supervisor. She speculated that perhaps the group's anxiety about the cause of his departure might be related to unprocessed feelings of guilt, that somehow they had been too much for him. Clearly some quite powerful dynamic was getting in the way of the functioning of the group and no doubt also appearing in the individual members' work with their clients.

Kathy decided to re-address the issue of the change of supervisor with the group, and also acknowledge that they might be concerned about their former supervisor and find the change difficult to manage for this reason. There wasn't a lengthy discussion – she kept in mind the main task, of supervision of their individual clients. But the members of the group seemed relieved, and it seemed as if this was the beginning of a change in the way the group functioned. In the course of the discussion, one member said 'we thought you didn't think much of us', an interesting confirmation of the depressed state of mind of the group but also something that made Kathy think about her own part in the development of this dynamic – perhaps she had been rather quick to make assumptions about them. She found herself acknowledging that perhaps she had been a disappointment. The group denied this, but subsequently presentations became more lively.

This example shows how particular circumstances and the resulting anxiety can lead to the development of basic assumption thinking in a group; it also highlights a systemic aspect of group supervision. The group dynamics had the effect of amplifying some anxieties that had their origins within individuals in the group, and were then experienced by all the members. As the supervisor, Kathy experienced these as a pressure to improve matters in a rather omnipotent way, by trying to do their thinking for them, or bring them to life.

It seemed likely in this case that the clients being worked with by the counsellors had also been affected by the dynamics in the group. We cannot be certain of the extent of this – the nature of the difficulties with the clients might have been unconsciously exaggerated in the service of making Kathy realise that something needed to be addressed (an example of projective identification as communication). But it can be seen that in this sense, the counsellors' clients are also part of the group, although not present in the room.

Pairing (baP)

This basic assumption is to do with hope for the future as a way of avoiding whatever seems difficult in the present, and is evident when two members of a group are seen to be in a particular type of relationship with each other, even if only momentarily. We can often recognise feelings of competition or concerns about being excluded when two people in a group pay attention to each other, but when basic assumption pairing is in operation this is not overtly the case – there will rather be an intense focus on the couple in the limelight. Bion says that the unconscious assumption under these circumstances is that the two people concerned, regardless of gender, have come together for sex, to generate a new leader – or a new idea – who will somehow solve all existing problems. For the hope to continue, this new state of affairs must always be in the future, since in reality perfection is impossible to obtain or sustain.

Sometimes, a supervision group will look to a particular couple to express this function, perhaps people who are thought to have particular valued attributes, or whose relationship is complex or has a somewhat unbounded quality. Any quality or relationship within the group that captures its attention is potential material for the basic assumption of pairing. Gosling (1981), writing about very small groups, notes that pairing is a common dynamic, often with different pairings developing within a very short space of time.

We can also apply this way of thinking to a counsellor–client pairing, that is being discussed in the group. Certain presentations can give rise to a feeling of specialness and engage the interest of others, even when it means that their own cases have less time for discussion. The example of Tom and his female client, considered later in the chapter, is a case in point. In this case, pairing seemed to be related to an aspect of the client – those in interesting or dramatic life situations or where there is an erotic transference often provide material which is reflected in the way the case is presented. The effect of focussing on a particular pair may be to bind anxiety about other aspects of the work or relationships in the group. It is worth noting because of the fact that it may divert needed attention from other apparently less interesting cases. In addition, such dynamics may indicate some form of parallel process whereby the concerns of the client or patient are being reflected in different ways within the group. We consider this situation in more detail later in the chapter.

Fight or flight (baF)

Bion's third basic assumption is that the group has met to fight something or alternatively to evade it by running away. A version of this is the tendency seen in many supervision groups to get a discussion going about things that are happening outside the group – criticising what is going on in other related settings can give the group a temporary feeling of solidarity and cohesion. Often what is being fought or evaded is insight and understanding, but it may also be to do with evading anxiety more directly. While it is common for the members of the group to band together against the outside world, it can also occur within groups; the following example shows group members avoiding their own anxiety at the expense of one member:

> *The supervision group comprised four counsellors in their second year of training, all working with one or two clients. One member of the group, Karen, had lost her first client after a few months and seemed likely to lose her second, a very depressed client. The client was missing sessions without warning and Karen was finding it hard to address this issue – when the client did appear, she felt relieved and did not want to disturb what she felt was a precarious equilibrium. (This seems quite a common dynamic when people begin working as counsellors – there is often an unconscious assumption that putting things into words will make things worse, not better.)*

The supervisor noted that there was a very competitive atmosphere within the group; they were all competent trainees, very focussed on getting through the course and accumulating their hours of counselling practice. Since the supervisor was the one responsible for allocating new clients as well as writing reports on their progress they wanted to impress her. The other three members of the group were doing fairly well in terms of keeping their current clients engaged with the work.

As time went on, it became apparent that Karen was being almost written off by other members of the group. Although seemingly sympathetic, they questioned her practice in various ways, asking questions about whether missed sessions counted in terms of 'hours' and wondering aloud who would get the next client. An enormous amount of attention seemed to be focussed on Karen's presentations, with apparently hypothetical questions being asked about 'whether it was wise to say this?', or 'how else might this issue be addressed?' and so on. Of course in one sense this sort of questioning attitude might be appropriate in a supervision group, but the supervisor noticed that other members did not get the same sort of scrutiny. Interestingly, the person who seemed to initiate some of these covert attacks was another member of the group, Marcia, who had also had difficulties in keeping her first client.

Things came to a head one day when Karen was due to present – she became quite overcome and needed a lot of encouragement to continue with the presentation. She said she felt a complete failure and wondered whether she should go on with the course. In fact the account of the session with her client showed that some changes were beginning to take place, both in the way she was working with the client and in his responses. The supervisor helped Karen and the group to realise this. In thinking about the work with the client, she also focussed on the way in which the client's feelings of inadequacy and despair were being put into and experienced by Karen. By focussing on the client's behaviour, she allowed the group to reflect that perhaps they had been quite lucky (so far) to avoid such a difficult client! She also said that it seemed as if Karen had more than her fair share of difficult feelings within the group. This had the effect of making the group somewhat more sympathetic and helpful in their interventions.

This situation could be seen as an example of a group working under the basic assumption fight/flight. It is of course quite usual for groups to be competitive but the supervisor's hypothesis was that the group, led by Marcia, had managed to get Karen to bear an undue share of the group's anxiety about the uncertainty inherent in therapeutic work. In this sense it was a flight away from the reality of the situation (that clients might leave or fail to attend, but in any case were not under the control of the counsellors) which they did not want to face as individuals. In the course of the flight, a sacrifice was needed; as Margaret Rioch (1975) writes '...in the fight/flight group there is no tolerance of sickness. Casualties are to be expected' (p. 26). As the above example shows, sometimes the supervisor may need to intervene to prevent casualties.

Bion's concept of valency

We might ask why or how a particular member of a group comes to be the subject of group pressures to take up a particular role. Bion uses the term 'valency' to describe a tendency within the individual which results in their behaviour fitting in with the current basic assumption. In the case of Karen, it seems that the behaviour of the client has led to her losing touch with her strengths, and that this worsening situation has led to her exposing her vulnerability within the group. It might be that she has a valency to be over submissive or masochistic, both with her client and with the group. This situation in turn has been seized on by the rest of the group, whether as the leader in the process or followers; participants with a valency for aggression and a tendency to mobilise it when anxious, such as Marcia, become dominant in fight/flight situations.

The concept of valency is a useful one since it allows us to think about the contribution of people's particular characteristics and tendencies when a group is operating in basic assumption mode. Scanlon (2002) gives a description of the way in which individuals with particular valencies might behave in a supervision group, not only towards the other members of the supervision group but also towards their patients. He writes that it is a crucial responsibility of the supervisor to 'help the supervisee to reflect upon his/her own valent tendencies' (p. 225). In this way they will be more able to avoid imposing their own difficulties, as reflected in basic assumption valencies, on the clients or patients that they are working with. In this context, Scanlon also writes about the importance of the supervision group in reflecting back to individual members something of the way in which they are experienced. He considers that this is one way of bridging the gap between the supervisee's 'espoused theory' (what they *imagine and say* they do in sessions) and their 'theory in use' (what they *actually* do).

So far we have considered mainly the regressive aspects of group behaviour, where anxiety leads to groups losing their focus on thinking about their clients or patients. The supervisor needs to be alert to this situation and take steps to counteract it. This can be done in various ways, from modelling a more reflective stance to taking steps to address the balance when one member seems to be getting more than their fair share of negative or positive feedback, as in the example of Karen above. When a particular state of mind seems to prevail in a group and the dynamics are affecting the task of supervision it may need addressing more actively. The danger of getting into a more interpretive stance is that we can get away from the main task of the group and collude with members' desires to turn the group into a therapy group, or scapegoat one member. This can happen, particularly when working with counsellors whose own therapy is not yet well established. It is a question of balance and supervisors need to find their own position as they reflect on their experience.

Parallel process and the work group

Assuming that the group is functioning fairly well as a work group, the dynamics of group supervision can be turned to good use in helping to develop an understanding of the clients. This is because, just as with individual supervision, the dynamics of the therapeutic relationship can be reflected, in various ways, within the group. Janet Mattinson (1975) was influential in applying the ideas of Searles, already considered in Chapter 4, to group situations. In her classic book *The Reflection Process in Casework Supervision* she gives vivid and engaging accounts of cases that were presented at workshops for supervisors of social workers which illustrate the way in which the dynamics of the case got reflected first in individual supervision and further in the case discussion workshop.

There seem to be two aspects of this process; one is that, as with individual supervision, unprocessed aspects of the transference and countertransference become clearer as the case is presented and thought about. An example that comes to mind is in Betty Joseph's (1983) paper 'Transference: the total situation'. She (op. cit., p. 158) describes a case discussion in a clinical seminar where initially it had been hard to understand what was going on with the patient in terms of the transference:

The seminar felt that many of the interpretations about this were sensitive and seemed very adequate. Then the seminar started to work very hard to understand more. Different points of view about various aspects were put forward, but no one felt quite happy about their own or other people's ideas. Slowly it dawned on us that probably this was the clue, that our problem in the seminar was reflecting the analyst's problem in the transference, and that what was probably going on in the transference was a projection of the patient's inner world, in which she, the patient could not understand and, more, could not make sense of what was going on. She was demonstrating what it felt like to have a mother who could not tune into the child, and, we suspected, could not make sense of the child's feelings either, but behaved as if she could, as we, the seminar, were doing.

This is a very subtle example of the process of the group throwing light on the patient's difficulties. A further aspect of the transference and countertransference being reflected in the group process comes about because of the different perspectives of the other members in the group – it is as though the group represents different aspects of the individual client, or the relationship. These can be a great help to the supervision process, and it also takes some of the pressure off the supervisor.

Various writers have commented on the value of a group's countertransference in assisting the therapist to develop ideas about the level and nature of disturbance in a patient. Christopher Bollas (2000, p. 176), contrasting neurotic patients with those with more perverse or psychotic difficulties, writes:

Hysterics can be frightening and paralysing, but even though the analyst may have a hard time thinking, such actions do not constitute the same attack on linking of which Bion writes. A great deal can be gleaned from a group's response to a clinical case presentation. Regardless of how mad the patient appears, if the group's response to the presentation is alive with ideas – interests, associations, links between contents, etc. – it is impossible for this to be a response to the borderline or perverse character. This is evidence, clinical evidence, of that type of kind of unconscious communication typical of the psychoneurotic personality.

He goes on to say that a perverse patient leaves the group feeling deadened, while presentations concerning a narcissistic patient tend to result in a sleepy atmosphere in the group. He considers that a more fragmented and anxious dynamic, with difficulties in thinking 'may be clinical evidence of the unconscious reception of a borderline personality'.

Being able to notice the different ways in which the group is reacting helps the inexperienced supervisee to get away from thinking only of the manifest content of sessions (see Chapters 2 and 5) and to develop a sense of the importance of the inner world of the client/patient, as reflected in the transference and countertransference. The following example illustrates this point:

> A group were discussing two of their clients, both with a history of violence and abuse in their families. First, Tom reported on his client, a young woman who was struggling to come to terms with the effect of this history on her sexual and emotional life. A break was approaching and the client was upset about this, although not admitting it. She was curious about Tom's break, but also let him know that she was being self destructive in various ways – she managed to get herself into a fight after getting very drunk, as well as failing to turn up for a vital exam. Tom was initially very worried about her.
>
> The discussion of this case sparked a great deal of interest and concern, as well as disapproval and sympathy for the client and her predicament, with different people in the group taking up different stances. The atmosphere was somewhat charged, veering towards the argumentative, and with various interruptions, but essentially creative in that a synthesis in understanding began to emerge. One person jokingly said, 'she clearly fancies you' and was surprised when the group took this seriously; further exploration did suggest an eroticized transference which Tom had ignored. But he was able to recognize it once it was pointed out, and related it to her feelings about her father's relationship with another woman. Tom also recognised that he hadn't addressed the issue of the break nearly enough. The supervisor also suggested that maybe the client's behaviour as reflected in the group was a way of avoiding much more difficult issues to do with her underlying depression and despair.
>
> The group moved on, reluctantly, to Judy's case. The issues presented were not so dissimilar; the report of the session contained material relating to abusive incidents in the client's life, and his concern that he would harm himself. From their manifest content, these ought to have been horrifying. However it seemed as if no one could really take them seriously, and the group relapsed into an introspective rather silent frame of mind. One member started yawning, various lines of enquiry were started and trailed out. A discussion developed about whether this client

*was 'really' at risk and someone pointed out that this conversation hap-
pened every time this client was discussed in the group. The discussion
did indeed have a ritualistic quality and the group concluded that perhaps this related to the way the client relied on a rather obsessional way
of thinking to distance himself from his hopeless feelings.*

This very simplified account illustrates Bollas's point about the
nature of disturbance and in this case the defences used to fight
depression, and shows how the supervision group's process can
be illuminating in opening up the discussion and deepening the
understanding about the nature of the therapeutic relationship. In
the first case, it seems as if the group's competitiveness and liveli-
ness, which was activated by the presentation, mirrored some of the
Oedipal difficulties of the client. With the second case, a more tentative understanding eventually developed. The group could see that
something of the dynamics of the session with the client had been
recreated within the group. The client's tendency in the sessions
was to disavow the intensity of his feelings by a sort of ritualised
approach to the way he expressed his concerns, so that his account
lacked a sense of urgency, and this found a resonance in the way
in which the group reflected on his case. These examples show the
importance of thinking about the group's reactions to presentations,
and suggests that often there is a part of the countertransference that
cannot immediately be processed and needs to be experienced, in
this case by the other members of the group. The supervisor needs
to stand back and allow the group to see what is unfolding, and also
show that they value these experiences as an aid to understanding.
This will allow the members of the group to make better use of their
countertransference when in sessions with their own clients.

Practical aspects of group supervision

So far we have considered aspects of group supervision in terms
of the underlying processes going on within the group, whether
related to issues with the membership or as a reflection of the
clients or patients being discussed. The way in which arrangements
for the group are thought about by the supervisor makes a great
deal of difference to the degree of containment that it can offer.
These will also depend on the setting and context for supervision
(which is the subject of the next chapter) as well as the supervisor's own job description, in terms of the role and responsibilities

they are expected to fulfil. As with individual supervision, there can be a tension between the educative and monitoring aspects of the supervisor's function.

Setting up a group

In the light of the discussion so far, it can be seen that the supervisor has an important influence on helping the group to function as a work group, where the main focus is on the clients and the discussion of process contributes to furthering understanding in this direction.

Groups like individuals need time to settle into supervision and there needs to be time to discuss boundaries and practices before clients are seen – it can be very disconcerting for supervisees to be rushed into this before they have had a chance to get to know the group, and since they do not feel well held, they may not be able to keep their clients. This applies to trainees in particular but also to an extent to more experienced therapists. It can seem awkward when a group of counsellors are waiting for clients; there can be a sense of being in limbo and a pressure to get started. Sometimes this can result in supervisors allocating clients or allowing work to begin before the group has properly established itself. As with individual supervision, the supervisor needs to be happy that the supervisees are ready to begin work with clients.

Sometimes there is a shortage of clients or patients, and in that case the supervisor needs to think how the waiting time should be spent. Group members may have ideas about this – there may be topics they want to discuss, or they can be asked to bring observations of accounts of situations which offer the opportunity for the group to apply psychodynamic thinking. Another possibility is to give the group suitably disguised case material or accounts of intake interviews to discuss; this also allows issues to do with confidentiality and ethics to be raised. All of these activities allows the supervisor to learn about the group members and their understanding and for the group to learn about the supervisor.

The situation often arises where some members of the group have clients and others do not; if this continues for any length of time it can be very painful for the one who has no client. Sometimes it results in the group member feeling silenced; I recall one member of a group saying, 'I feel sorry for myself when they are presenting. I come to feel I have nothing to say – how can I know anything?'

Others in this situation react by taking rather too much space and constantly chipping in with their ideas. Sometimes there is a flight into theory, as a substitute for the experience of being with a client. The supervisor needs to be alert to these ways of expressing anxiety and their effect on the individual and group dynamics.

The supervisor has to think about how many members the group should have; this may be related to the level of experience of the participants but the length of time for each session of the group and the frequency of meeting are clearly relevant. It has been suggested that the numbers of patients or clients being discussed in the group is a more relevant constraint than the numbers of supervisees; the supervisor needs to be able to bring them to mind, with prompting, particularly if they are also responsible for their clinical management. For new supervisees and where group supervision is the only form of supervision, I would suggest that the equivalent of at least half an hour a week per supervisee is needed.

Supervisors vary in the way in which they allocate the time on a week-by-week basis; this may partly depend on the function of the group in terms of the balance between educational and monitoring needs. Where the supervisor is clinically responsible for the cases under discussion there is more need to enquire on a week by week basis how things are going, particularly if the group is relatively new to the work. Where this is not the case, and the group members are experienced practitioners, the group can be run more as a case discussion group, focussing on one case in detail. By a case discussion group I mean a group who have met to increase their overall understanding of therapeutic work, often as part of a training in counselling or psychotherapy course. Usually in this situation one member of the group will present their case, in some detail, and there will be a joint exploration of the material and the ideas it generates. Such a group can be free from the need to monitor the work on a week by week basis, and can have a more relaxed, generally educational remit. In contrast, a supervision group will normally have a more focussed approach, with the supervisor having some responsibility for the course of the clinical work if group members are trainees. This implies an attention to the monitoring function of supervision and a preparedness to offer suggestions and guidance as necessary depending on how the work is going, just as we do in individual supervision.

For supervisees who are new to therapeutic work and new to the group, it seems important to offer some space every time the group meets. As we have seen in Chapter 2, trainees at the beginning of their career are not yet confident about being able to contain their own or the client's anxiety, and it can be a great relief to be able to talk, albeit briefly, about what has transpired in the sessions. They are still functioning at what Hawkins and Shohet (op. cit.) term the 'self centred stage' when their main preoccupation is in terms of their own progress, and they realise that they are dependent on the judgement of the supervisor to understand how things are going (see Chapter 4 of this book). But as they get more experienced they become more able to contain their concerns and present at less frequent intervals. Many supervisors operate a combination of approaches, with some space for matters that seem urgent followed by a more detailed consideration of individual cases. But we need to make sure that the time allocated for individual cases does not get hijacked by supervisees whose cases are always 'urgent' – this is one way in which the competitiveness of the group can get expressed.

Supervisors also need to ensure that they have time to process the content of presentations; it is easy to feel overwhelmed by the amount of material that a group can generate. It may be necessary to put a time limit on presentations to allow time for reflection and discussion. It can sometimes be useful to have the presenter be silent for 10 minutes or so following the presentation to give others a chance to respond.

A further dimension in running a group is the question of the range of experience and ability of its members. One of the advantages of groups where some members are more experienced is that the others can learn from them, but sometimes an unhelpful dynamic can develop where the newest member is always treated as the younger sibling who has to be looked after. As Gosling (1981) has pointed out, small groups often recreate family dynamics. This may also mean that apparently more experienced supervisees put their own needs on hold, getting into difficulties because the group and the supervisor are working on the assumption that they are doing fine. While it may seem mechanistic to divide the time absolutely equally, regardless of numbers of clients or experience, we clearly need to pay attention to time allocation, in the interests of managing competition in the group and ensuring that all the clients or patients – and not only the most 'interesting' or worrying ones – get their share of space. I think it is also important to remember that the most inexperienced counsellor has something to contribute in group supervision, because they are able to take a different perspective from the person presenting the session.

It can be difficult to manage the giving of feedback in a group situation, particularly when there are differing levels of experience and ability. The supervisor has to steer a path between challenging the supervisee appropriately while not allowing or perpetuating a situation where one member always seems to be in the firing line. Clearly tact is required in terms of commenting on individual presentations; when it comes to periodic reviews of trainees' work, it is usually better to set aside time for individual meetings, which allow for a franker discussion. Other circumstances need to be thought through as they arise.

A group member had been taken to task by the manager of an organisation for not keeping appropriate records; the penalty was that he had to see a further client before qualifying. The supervisor had talked with him on the telephone; he felt humiliated and ashamed. He asked that the matter should not be mentioned in the group except in terms of his taking on a further client. This seemed entirely reasonable to the supervisor, and engendered a much more positive attitude in the supervisee.

Institutional influences on group functioning

So far we have considered the possible dynamics of a group as a group, but since supervision groups usually meet in an organisational context, this will also influence the way the group interacts and uses supervision. We need to be alert to pressures from the supervisees to use us in a particular way and create splits within the organisation. We also have to monitor the effects on our own behaviour, of our own position in relation to the organisation.

A supervisor running an (external) supervision group for a counselling service invited the supervisees to talk of any concerns they might have about the organisation and the way in which it affected them. The supervisor was expected to take some responsibility for monitoring their progress, so this might have been considered part of the role. In practice however, the supervisor discovered that the supervisees tended to use this opportunity to complain about other settings on the courses. He had to point out that there were other places where these issues could be addressed. This meant resisting the temptation to set himself up as a good object, or gratify his own curiosity. Of course he also needed to consider whether these complaints related to the group itself, and his management of it.

Groups, like individuals, are subject to pressures arising from the context of the work, in particular the nature of the patients of clients with whom members are working. The following example, contributed by a colleague, relates to a supervision group set up to support care workers and other staff working in a nursing home for elderly patients.

The supervisor was struck by the fact that very often one particular carer, Eva, would apparently doze off once the meeting got going. It became a source of embarrassed amusement to her colleagues; they knew she was working very hard at her college course. The other members of the group seemed alert and very engaged considering the nature of the work they were doing, which was often arduous, both physically and emotionally, and at times demoralising. They had to face, on a day-to-day basis, the sadness of the increasing physical and mental deterioration, and eventual death, of successive intakes of their elderly residents. The supervisor could see that perhaps Eva was expressing some of the carers' depression about the work and the institution, and the sleepiness might be a way of blocking out more difficult thoughts. His first thoughts about the situation, therefore, related to the role that Eva might be playing in the group, allowing the others to maintain a more lively stance. But then he also realised that Eva's sleepiness could be mirroring the often soporific atmosphere of the residents' lounge, and the way in which residents would by degrees become increasingly withdrawn, spending a lot of their time asleep.

The subject of the influence of the client or patient on supervising in institutional contexts will be further explored in the next chapter.

Summary and conclusions

In this chapter we have thought about the particular characteristics of group supervision. Working in groups creates particular anxieties which we have considered in the light of Bion's ideas on the three kinds of basic assumption groups. Supervising groups often requires a nice balance between taking account of these dynamics and focussing on the work with clients or patients, but we have seen that there are situations when acknowledging difficulties within the group can create space for focusing on the main task.

We have also thought about they way in which the dynamics relating to the client or patient can be reflected in the group processes; in this way group supervision can give an extra dimension to understanding the dynamics of the therapeutic encounter. The chapter concludes with some ideas about setting up and running groups. There is always a tension between individual and group needs which needs to be thought about in terms of the arrangements made for the group.

Some thoughts to emerge from this chapter are summarised below:

- Because groups are bound to stimulate a particular kind of anxiety in the individual, there is likely to be an increased use of mechanisms such as projection and projective identification by the members, as well as feelings of envy and competition. There can also be a fear of shame and humiliation. The group supervisor needs to be aware of these tendencies and the pressure they can put on the members of the group, including the supervisor.
- Such pressures incline towards action rather than reflection and this, combined with the fact that there is usually a great deal of material to get through in a supervision group, means that the group supervisor has to take up their role with authority, to create a space for thinking about the work.
- The supervisor of a group, even more than in individual supervision, needs to think about the issue of containment and the way in which this is provided in the arrangements for the setting up and running of the group.
- On a positive note, a supervision group that is working well can allow information about transference and countertransference in the therapy setting to be brought to the surface, through being reflected in group dynamics. The atmosphere can also be very supportive to individuals – this is the rewarding and stimulating side of supervising groups.

7

SUPERVISING WORK IN INSTITUTIONS

Introduction

So far we have considered aspects of individual supervision as well as those to do with working with groups of supervisees. While we have sometimes indicated context, we have not focussed to any extent on the impact of this on the work of supervision. This is the subject of this chapter, which focuses on aspects of supervising those working in institutions.

Whether counselling is the main focus of activity or complementary to the main functions of the institution, providing psychotherapy or counselling in an institutional setting often challenges the therapist's assumptions about boundaries and ways of working. This in turn may create dilemmas for the supervisor; we may find that our ideas about good practice are being challenged by the demands of the institution, as experienced by our supervisees – for example, the need to work very short term, or arrange sessions without regular time boundaries, or to share confidential information with others. We may find that we have to justify the need for supervision, or that when staff are under pressure supervision sessions get cancelled or not attended, because other work is considered more urgent.

As those working in the National Health Service (NHS) or in educational settings cannot fail to be aware, there have been profound cultural changes over the last two decades, associated with changing ways of funding these services, which result in constant challenges to ways of working. William Halton, writing in 1995, highlights the fact that a culture of competition has replaced the dependency culture that is in many respects more appropriate to the primary tasks of educating and caring for the health needs of the population. His paper details the many effects of these changes on the organisation and their employees. He considers that, while some take the view that the introduction of market forces has brought benefits, those working in these environments may feel a sense of loss and become demoralised and overwhelmed, as the pressure on resources increases, and their ability to provide what they consider is needed is undermined. These trends have continued.

In higher education, for example, financial constraints have often resulted in the cutting back or elimination of ancillary services such as counselling provision, as universities struggle to survive in a competitive climate where getting the maximum number of students through their course becomes the priority. In turn the students are in survival mode; many are having to work several days a week to finance their courses. In the NHS, the introduction of the internal market together with an increasing need to consider the patient as a consumer means that services have to demonstrate their effectiveness and competence – there is a need for constant monitoring and measurement, as to whether various targets are being met. These pressures often have implications for the type – and by extension the quality – of work that can be done in counselling and psychotherapy services. In addition, those working psychodynamically face competition from therapeutic modes such as cognitive behavioural therapy (CBT) where it is easier to measure results in terms of the stated aims.

These changes have impacted on the counsellor working within an institution, who is likely to have additional responsibilities having, for example, a monitoring or management role; this may involve promoting the service to other parts of the organisation, providing support for other parts of the organisation, and supervising trainees. While these roles may not necessarily be the main subject for supervision, the way in which they are managed may impact on the work with clients. Some of us with experience of thinking in an institutional context may be happy to move towards a more consultative role in supervision in these circumstances. It may in fact be considered as part of our job description, if we are working within the institution. Even if this is not the case, it may be necessary to be able to think with our supervisees about the organisational dynamics. The danger of expanding our role in this way is that sometimes the work with individual clients can get lost.

I will begin by considering perspectives which can be applied to organisations, and how they can help us to put supervision work in context. One of these, the psychoanalytic perspective, is very familiar to readers, and we can apply this thinking to institutions. Group relations perspectives and systems theory as applied to organisations can also contribute to the thinking of those working in institutions. In practice, concepts from all of these theoretical standpoints are often interwoven; aspects of these different perspectives taken together can enrich understanding.

Understanding organisational dynamics: psychoanalytic and group relations perspectives

In the previous chapter we considered the fact that groups, although made up of individuals, can have an emotional life of their own. The same is true of organisations, and some of the ideas about the emotional life of organisations relate to the work done by Bion and others in relation to groups. They have a common background in the ideas of Klein and her development of theories about defences against anxiety.

The work of Isobel Menzies Lyth has drawn attention to the way in which organisations can defend against anxiety, very often that provoked by aspects of the main purpose of the institution. In her ground-breaking study (1960) of a nursing service in a general hospital she considered the particular nature of the anxiety generated by the task of nursing, which she thought related to the strong and often conflicting feelings aroused by working with ill and dying people and their relatives. She showed that the hospital had developed ways of working which, at least initially, allowed the nurses to tolerate the anxiety inherent in nursing; these ways of working had become embedded in procedures and had taken on a life of their own. These included, for example, dividing the work up into a series of discrete tasks, which could be performed by any member of the team for all the patients on the ward, the aim being to prevent attachments developing between individual nurses and patients.

However, a price was paid in terms of the level of the nurses' job satisfaction, and staff turnover rates were high. Unhappy relations existed between the different levels of the hierarchies that accompanied this particular way of working. And because responsibility for tasks was spread so diffusely, with a complex system of checks and balances, individuals were not able to take or enjoy responsibility for their work. As Hinshelwood and Skogstad (2000) point out in their concluding reflections on health care structures, the underlying (unconscious) assumptions built into the institution being studied by Menzies Lyth were firstly that 'if one remains emotionally distant from patients, one won't feel anxiety on their behalf', and secondly, that guilt is avoided by passing responsibility for decisions to someone else (p. 156).

In medical settings where professionals are working constantly with the reality that their patients may die, it may be very difficult – because too painful – to keep in mind the emotional needs of the patient. In this context the supervisor or consultant's role may be to keep this in mind. Margaret Cohen (2003), writing of her experience as a child psychotherapist in a neonatal intensive care unit, thinks about and articulates very movingly the experience of the babies staying in the unit. She also writes of the ways in which the staff inevitably defend against the terrible anxiety of working with such ill babies and their traumatised parents, for example, by seeing themselves as the healthy adult ones and the families they are working with as passive and lacking in resources (p. 59). Under these circumstances it may become difficult for staff to use such support that is available, because it throws them into what they may consider to be a dangerously vulnerable state of mind.

Working with the other end of the age range also presents challenges. As Paul Terry (2008) writes, working with the elderly inevitably brings the realisation that we are helpless to ameliorate physical decline or prevent death, including of course our own death, and this helplessness may make it particularly difficult to face organisational changes. He writes of the functions that support groups may fulfil, in giving staff working in care roles a space to understand the emotional experience of working in such settings, as well as helping them to think about their patients' feelings (pp. 139–149).

In such situations a supervisor acting as a consultant to groups of staff has to be able to provide a space where these very difficult issues can be faced – which includes being prepared to work with the intrinsic difficulty of such meetings taking place at all. And even in areas where the primary task does not always involve such life and death issues, it seems to be a common experience that offers may be refused; meetings are set up, and apparently welcomed, but no one turns up – or future meetings are cancelled.

A counsellor in a university setting was asked to meet with student midwives, who had asked for help in 'stress management'. She developed a plan for a meeting which included thinking about the nature of issues that midwives might have to face. One complication that came up before the meeting was that the tutor who had asked for the meeting wanted to attend and was disconcerted when the counsellor suggested that the midwives might speak more freely if she was not there – however, she agreed to be absent.

The meeting itself started slowly, people drifted in late clutching coffee cups (their lunch hour had been cut short). Once they started talking, it was clear that these students were not used to thinking about the emotional impact of their work in this setting. However, they did seem to appreciate the opportunity being provided. To begin with they talked rather angrily of how hard they were made to work on the course. After a while they moved to talking about the 'life and death' aspects of the work, one talking movingly of how affected she'd been by a recent stillbirth, others about the impact of doing this work on their own family life. They conveyed a sense of the responsibility that they all felt, and of how much they needed support to do this work.

The meeting was considered a success initially and plans were made for future meetings. But then the counsellor had a phone call from the tutor – an extra seminar has been put into the timetable and the meeting was put on hold.

It wasn't clear to the counsellor what had happened; when she first thought about the situation she felt cheated and was inclined to be angry with the tutor, but maybe the students had also found the meeting too difficult, since it had appeared as an isolated event on their agenda. It is interesting that the material in the session about stillbirths also resonates with the premature termination of the meetings for the midwives. There might be many factors contributing to this situation in this case, which illustrates the way groups in organisations can move towards thinking about painful dynamics but then retreat; it is very hard to maintain a position of vulnerability when your daily work involves such serious issues. Supervisors working with those offering this sort of support have to help them to withstand the constant uncertainty and the feeling of being rebuffed; if events can be placed in the context of institutional dynamics it becomes more bearable, because less personal.

There can be a tendency for counselling and psychotherapy services working within institutions to consider themselves immune from such dynamics, but we all make use of such defences as denial, splitting and idealisation, and projective identification, and these become institutionalised in terms of the organisation of the work. We can think of different parts of the organisation as operating as a system of groups and affected by similar dynamics to those described in the previous chapter. In any organisation where counselling or therapy plays a part, the emotional and mental difficulties of the clients or patients are bound to create anxiety. This will often be offloaded from one group of professionals to another. The way in which these projective processes will be played out in practice will depend partly on the context in which the service is situated, whether it is a service attached to a larger organisation (e.g., staff counselling services within businesses or in the NHS) or a service set up with the provision of psychotherapy or counselling as its main purpose.

Take, for example, the case of counselling services within educational institutions. There will often be the (largely unconscious) expectation that the counselling service will deal with all the troublesome members of the institution so that the real work or task of the institution can continue uninterrupted elsewhere. But the service may choose to deal with this in different ways. Sometimes there are parallels with the situation described in the Menzies Lyth study above, where a morass of rules and procedures is set up with the aim of dispelling anxiety about the distress and disturbance that some members of the institution may experience. In the need to stick obsessively to procedures and fulfil administration expectations, the client's needs may get lost:

> A supervisee, Gavin, talked of the demands being made of him by his (non counselling) line manager. Exams were approaching and this always placed a heavy demand for the service; nevertheless the manager had chosen this time to demand a lengthy report on the way in which a new monitoring system was working. The supervisee felt desperate; referrals to the service were well up, as they always were at this time of the year. Students were being asked to wait for four weeks for an appointment, by which time term would have ended. The manager said that he too was under pressure, from the Dean of students – he really needed the information. Gavin felt that there was no flexibility in this case, despite his protests, and he felt undermined in his ability to do what he thought of as his proper job. That was the initial impression that the supervisor had, anyway.
>
> Further exploration however revealed that Gavin was in some ways quite glad of the chance to get away from working with students. 'The pressure seems relentless' he said, 'sometimes it's almost too much to bear. I find them so demanding. Of course I know I'm exaggerating. But taking a day off to write the report seems quite attractive compared with the alternative, at this time of the year.'

Gavin thought about his position; he realised that he was avoiding the anxiety engendered by the increased contact with disturbed and distressed students by agreeing to prioritise non contact work, identifying with the manager rather than the client group. Of course he knew he needed to provide the information for his manager, but he also thought about ways of making his workload more bearable, in terms of organising the workload with his colleagues.

Sometime the opposite situation develops, and the counsellor gets overly preoccupied by the demands of clinical work, which then tends to be idealised as a way of avoiding thinking about wider issues, as in the following example:

> Martha was a counsellor who had just started working part time in a higher education setting. As the only counsellor on a particular campus, she had come, even in a short time, to represent the counselling service in peoples' minds and since she was an effective and helpful practitioner she was inundated with demands for appointments. There was a high level of anxiety on the campus – a student had committed suicide a few months earlier, resulting in an increase of seriously disturbed students being referred by tutors. She knew that she was seeing far more students in a day than was really feasible, using up all her lunch hour and administration time to cram in emergency appointments. In fact she seldom came out of her consulting room.
>
> Martha told her supervisor how she had gone into work that morning to find a panicky answer phone message from an administrator, to the effect that she needed to ring back straight away. It ended with the words, 'well, I suppose if you're not there now it's no bloody good anyway ...' She had followed up this phone call to discover that a student had come into the central admin office and become psychotic, shouting and behaving in a threatening manner, and no one had known what to do. In the event an ambulance had been called and the student had been taken to hospital. However, it was clear that the underlying assumption was that dealing with students in this condition was the counsellor's job. She had felt guilty and apologetic.
>
> When this matter was discussed in supervision, Martha realised that she had somehow become idealised, as someone who would always be available to manage difficult situations relating to mental health problems, perhaps so that others did not have to face the knowledge of the extent of the students' disturbances. Then when a crisis developed and she did not meet people's expectations, of course, her (non counselling) colleagues were furious with her.

It is worth considering the influence of the institutional dynamics in this case. It seems that the administrator, faced with a student who was clearly out of touch with reality, had absorbed some of his panic and distress and finding no help available had passed some of these feelings on to Martha with her angry message, who in turn had felt very hurt by the administrator's anger.

The supervisor considered the matter; in these crises it is tempting to take sides and allocate blame, and initially she felt inclined to sympathise with Martha, who was torn between being over responsible and at the same time feeling that she was being unjustly treated. But the roots of this type of polarised thinking are complex. Some may lie in the individual; maybe Martha needed to look at her own valency for taking on too much. Vega Roberts (1994b), writing of the 'self assigned impossible task', points out that while consciously those in the helping professions may be motivated by idealism, this is likely to be associated with a less conscious need to effect reparation, linked to guilt relating to our destructive potential. These dynamics are carried over from our very earliest experiences, and acting them out can result in overwork and burnout; failure is almost inevitable because of the unrealistic expectations that have been generated.

However, the supervisor was also aware that, in the existing educational climate, there were increasing pressures for the university to take on vulnerable students who were on the boundaries of being able to manage the demands of degree courses. (In this case the psychotic student represented, at every level, a failure on the part of the institution, and there was an urgent need to get someone – in this case the counsellor – to take on responsibility, to assuage unconscious guilt and to remove such a disturbing presence from the institution.) Then she became more aware of the reality of the difficult situation that the administrator had been facing.

The supervisor said that she thought the administrator's feelings, of there being no help available, needed to be taken seriously – it had clearly been a very frightening situation. (She could empathise with the distressed administrator – not to mention the distressed student – as well as her supervisee.) She could see that on a practical level, the counselling service needed to find ways of supporting those coming into contact with students in crisis. Martha also needed to clarify her own limits and boundaries, to give realistic information on how she could help.

Reflecting on this, Martha thought about the containment she was trying to offer to the university, on behalf of the counselling service; she realised that some of this function could be provided by her contribution to thinking about the best way to handle such crises. As a part time lone counsellor, she could not possibly offer a full time crisis intervention service – but she could make sure everyone had access to information on the best way of handling such events, as well as offer emotional support to those affected.

These two examples show counsellors coping with anxiety by adopting very different tactics – in one case, becoming somewhat anesthetised to distress and on the other getting overwhelmed by it. Of course counselling and therapy services exist in organisations to help the institution manage distress and disturbance, and part of the supervisor's task under these circumstances, in addition to supervising clinical work, is to help the counsellor draw appropriate boundaries and provide a thoughtful psychodynamic input to institutional thinking.

The organisation in the mind

From the examples above, it is clear that the supervisor working with therapists and counsellors based in an institution needs to be curious about the nature of the setting and aspects of the culture of the organisation, as experienced by the supervisee. Part of the experience could be expressed as the transference – or countertransference – of the supervisee to the institution, but using these terms in this context does not convey the complexity of the experience. We need to consider the 'organisation in the mind' of the supervisee. This term, originally introduced by Pierre Turquet in a group relations context, has come to refer to the way in which the behaviour of members of an organisation in relation to each other is influenced by their (often unconscious) fantasies and assumptions that they hold about the organisation. David Armstrong, elaborating on this concept (2005), writes of the way in which an individual's emotional experience relates to and resonates with that of the organisation as a whole. In turn this is a function of the interrelations between task, structure, culture and context (op. cit., pp. 5–9) drawing on psychoanalytic and systems theories.

The contribution of systems theory

We have considered systemic influences in supervision earlier in this book, in terms of thinking about the way in which dynamics relating to supervision can be transmitted to the therapy setting and vice versa, but systems theory is also a useful framework for thinking about the complexities of institutional functioning. (For an account of the approach, see, e.g., Vega Roberts 'The organisation of work' (1994a) or Miller and Rice (1967)). It can help us understand the role that counselling and other helping professions play in the workings of an organisation, as well as the boundaries between different groups or parts of the organisation.

As applied to organisations, open systems theory considers the institution in terms of its primary (main) task. The process of carrying out this task requires inputs (raw materials, employees and other resources) and results in an output. If circumstances change and resources become scarce, the functioning of the organisation is clearly going to be affected. Organisations, like living organisms, need to be adaptable to change.

A familiar example is the case of voluntary counselling organisations that often run into trouble when for one reason or another original sources of funds dry up. Sometimes the solutions adopted may make survival less likely, particularly if they are piecemeal rather than a more radical consideration of realities. For example, a service under financial pressure may start charging their clients – or increase their charges – for sessions, and then discover that fewer clients come to the service. This makes it less attractive as a centre for volunteer counsellors using the service to get experience, and makes it harder to fund other necessary inputs such as supervision.

Supervisors need to be able to acknowledge the way in which organisational characteristics and changes impact on their supervisee's work. The external realities are important, but so also is the interaction between these and the supervisee's experience. In other words, they need to think about the organisation in the mind of the supervisee – and then be able to think with the supervisee about the role they are playing, consciously or unconsciously, in the institution's work. Counselling and other support services come into being to help the institution fulfil its primary task, but as the examples above show, different parts of the organisation may have different views of the primary task, even at a conscious level, and at a deeper level, expectations may be quite at variance.

Of relevance here is Gordon Lawrence's conception of the different kinds of primary tasks (quoted by Vega Roberts op. cit., 1994a, p. 30) which allow an idea of the unconscious dynamics to be thought about within a systemic framework. There is a formal or official task, which he names the *normative primary task*. This is the task as defined in job descriptions and information on the functions of departments; it is the task in the public domain, as it were, even if it is not always kept in mind. But in addition there is the work that people believe they are carrying out – the *existential task* – which relates more to the idea of the organisation in the mind, described above. The *phenomenal task* is that which can be inferred from some-one's behaviour – we do not always know how our actions are interpreted by others. These distinctions can draw attention to the difference between the stated aims of an organisation and the often unconscious assumptions that are guiding attitudes and behaviour. As we have suggested, very often there is a desire that counselling services manage all the disturbance in an institution, an idea clearly contraindicated by the resources made available to them. Confusion about tasks and roles is often a source of conflict.

Parallel processes at an institutional level

Theories about systemic processes in an organisation also incorporate the idea that the nature of the primary task influences the dynamics. Naomi Stewart (2004), writing about supervising counsellors working in primary care, gives a vivid picture of the conditions in these settings, the sense of urgency and pressures in terms of number of patients and the way in which competition for scarce resources by professionals as well as envy of the counsellor' special role in the practice can result, for example, on attacks on boundaries in the form of counselling rooms being taken over at short notice. As we have already suggested, in health care settings manic defences are likely to come in to play to defend against the realties of working with seriously ill or dying patients. She points out that in supervision, counsellors may present confused and uncertain accounts of their work, and this must be understood as being related to chaotic aspects of the setting. The supervisor must take in this confusion (which is part of the organisation in the mind of the supervisee) and then create a more bounded opportunity for supervisees to recover their capacity for thinking about the patients. This will then impact on the way in which supervisees can educate the organisation about their needs.

The following example shows among other things the influence of the client group on the way a problem manifested itself in supervision, and was also acted out in the counselling setting.

A supervisee who had taken over the management of a counselling service working mainly with young people brought an account of an ongoing problem with her colleagues. She had been concerned for some time to get the counsellors working in the service, for whom she had line management responsibility, to share certain administrative and service development tasks. The problem was, they simply would not do as she asked; she had tried everything, but it seemed that they could not accept that these tasks were part of their job description, (which they were) preferring instead to focus on their individual work. This was indeed their main task, but of course no counselling service can afford to ignore its interface with the outside world, and my supervisee thought she was being left with more than her fair share of this work. (In the terms we have been using above, we can see that there were different views of the balance between different aspects of the primary tasks of the service, as well as a disregard for her authority.)

She was clearly exasperated and I thought also somewhat scornful of the contribution that these counsellors, many of whom were older than her, were making to the service. Clearly they were not thinking 'institutionally' but it also seemed as my supervisee didn't feel confident about any aspect of their work. As she saw it, they reacted to her requests with a variety of somewhat literal, concrete ways of looking at the situation, almost as though they were deliberately missing the point, showing no evidence of a capacity to think and reflect. As a result she was having to do a great deal of the administrative and outreach work herself and was furious with them all.

There was a sense of their presenting a united front against her and she felt isolated, lonely and increasingly desperate. Listening to her, I felt the need first to empathise – and it did seem as if she was faced with a number of colleagues who were behaving in an intractable, obstinate way. There was a sense of something more, however. I began to feel somewhat identified with these older colleagues, as though I wasn't being much help either. I think I made some comment to this effect. I had earlier found myself making suggestions as to how she might approach the issue, which were firmly repudiated. I had the sense that my supervisee was rejecting what I had to offer in a rather literal way; discussions didn't seem to be leading anywhere. At times I was uncertain of whether what I was saying was being heard, but mainly my feelings were of being deskilled.

Soon afterwards my supervisee told me that she was not finding supervision helpful at the moment. She thought I was too prescriptive and was not really helping her with the pressures she was under. What she wanted was a space to think. This was what I hoped I was

providing, so to begin with I felt quite irritated. On reflection how-
ever, it seemed to me that the possibility of thinking had become reduced
at times in the previous few months. When we looked at the situa-
tion together I could see that I had failed to acknowledge sufficiently
the desperation in her position and the pressure she was under, partly
because of feeling defensive about not providing what was apparently
needed.

We considered certain idiosyncratic aspects of our relationship as
supervisor and supervisee, and this discussion gave us both something
to think about. But it later became clear that this issue also had roots in
the dynamics of the institution.

At a subsequent session, my supervisee arrived feeling very bruised,
reporting a violent verbal onslaught by one of the counsellors at a
meeting. She had been mercilessly criticized in front of a number of col-
leagues, in a way that had clearly been unbounded, unreasonable and
unprofessional. She had managed not to retaliate, realizing that this
behaviour was quite out of order and spoke for itself.

Discussion of this episode in supervision made us realise that some-
thing of the dynamics of the preoccupations of the young clients –
including their attitudes to authority and the way in which violent
feelings were acted out – was being reflected in the team dynamics,
and then subsequently, in a much more moderate way, in supervision
with me.

This realisation gradually paved the way for a different approach to
the problem, involving the whole team in thinking together with an
outside consultant about the way in which they worked together.
I continued to provide individual supervision for the supervisee.
This dual approach proved much more fruitful. This example is
also an illustration of the fact that the supervisor in these circumstances needs to be aware of other resources that might be more
appropriate to the situation, as well as their own boundaries and limitations to the role of supervisor in this context. In addition of course,
this vignette raises questions about the direction of influence of the
dynamics involved. At first sight it seems as if I was on the receiving
end of something that originated with the adolescent client group.
But there was a reality to the events in supervision, and perhaps
I was also modelling a less constructive way of working with colleagues, for my supervisee. I certainly experienced the criticisms of
the subordinates, reported by my supervisee, as relating to me. This
is an illustration of the situation mentioned in Chapter 4, that Langs
(op. cit.) writes about; it will be remembered that he considered

that the patient's reported statements should first be considered as applying to the supervisory situation.

Common dynamics in supervising work in institutions

As we have seen, counsellors working in institutions have to keep a balance between getting caught up in the sometimes unthinking demands of others in the organisation and retreating to a more isolated position, clinging to standards that may be impossible to maintain. Supervisors need to help their supervisee navigate between these two positions, between privileging action rather than thinking and being overwhelmed by the demands of a overactive superego.

The supervisor also needs to be aware of the effect of these pressures in the supervision session. Sometimes we can find ourselves manoeuvred into representing a position that is in opposition to the ethos and values of the organisation, and this is not in the long run helpful to the supervisee. I set out below some common aspects of institutional work and dynamics, as they can appear in supervision.

Different concepts of boundaries: the nature of the contract

Supervisors working primarily in private practice, or in settings where clients or patients are seen for a year or more or in an open-ended contract, may find themselves challenged when supervisees present work that is more short term, time limited, or of necessity involves shorter, ad hoc counselling sessions. Supervisors need a somewhat different approach to the work, in the sense that the constraints of the setting need to be understood. For example, bereavement counsellors often visit their clients in their own homes, and this calls for a particular focus on boundaries.

In the NHS counsellors often work in outpatient clinics where counselling is offered on demand to those patients where it is felt that there is an emotional aspect of a physical problem that may need to be addressed urgently. A woman attending a clinic for termination of pregnancy may not feel able to return on a different day for an appointment with a counsellor – it may be more appropriate for her to be seen after her medical appointment. If further sessions are needed it can be quite difficult to move from the urgency of the clinic situation where someone is seen immediately to a more bounded, even if short term, contract. But in supervision also, the supervisor needs to work with the supervisee on what are the essential aspects of the setting that need to be retained, and where there can be a compromise.

Brief work

Often short-term work (however this is defined) is the usual form of treatment in community counselling agencies, universities and primary health care practices. If supervisors are to be helpful to those working in these settings, they need to have worked on their own understanding of the limitations and opportunities of short term work, both in terms of what can be done and the type of clients or patients that can be helped.

Gillian Ingram (2003), working in a university context and writing about the nature of therapeutic time, makes the point that working short term is a very powerful way of helping therapists and clients to face up to the painful realities of ending as well as the opportunities for growth and development. There is a need for the counsellor to accept their guilt and sadness at not providing more for the client, if they are to work effectively with just a few sessions. This also implies a role for supervisors; we need to support our supervisees in working to a time-limited contract, and not undermine them by conveying an idea that it is likely to be second best. (We may still need to help supervisees think about who is most likely to benefit from brief counselling, and who to refer for longer term work.)

Alex Coren, in his book *Short-Term Psychotherapy* (2001), devotes a chapter to training and supervision of short-term therapy. One of the central tenets of his book is that short-term therapy has a knowledge base of its own; it is not simply a watered-down version of psychoanalytic therapy, and requires quite different skills from the therapist. He goes on to consider the role of supervision in this context, in terms of support and helping the therapist maintain an active focus in the sessions (pp. 187–192) outlining a number of points for supervisors to take into account. Supervision needs to mirror the conditions that the therapist experiences in clinical work, another instance of parallel process in supervision.

Confidentiality

Supervisors can often help think about the demands or requests for information that come the way of those working in institutions. To people outside the profession, aspects of the counselling frame may not be well understood.

A counsellor working in a further education college was approached by the deputy head with the comment that she needed more information about the work of the service. It would be useful if he could simply give her a list of all the students currently receiving counselling. The counsellor felt this was quite unacceptable and said so, to the annoyance of the deputy head.

When it was discussed in supervision, it was suggested that this demand had its roots in an anxiety that academic staff would fail to distinguish students who were struggling emotionally from those who had more prosaic reasons for not working well on their courses. The worry was about unwittingly making matters worse for these students, and not simply about wanting to be in control of sources of information (which was what the counsellor had thought initially). The supervisory role in this case included thinking with the supervisee about compromise positions, including the possibility, in certain circumstances, of asking students for consent to let others know there was a problem. (This was something that already happened when students wanted deferrals or other special consideration.) Some time later, the counsellor also reported that he had started providing more general information about the activities of the counselling service, and this seemed to be welcomed; it was possible to be more cooperative while still maintaining boundaries.

A different view of transference

Earlier in this chapter, we considered the idea of the 'organisation in the mind' as applied to those working in an institution. We have seen that there may be discrepancies between the given (normative task) and unconscious assumptions about roles and tasks, both our own and other people's. This applies not only to our supervisees, but also to those they are working with, including the clients. This means that the transference may be to the institution or the counselling service as a part of the institution, rather than operating on a more personal level.

The following example shows the way in which a student client's transference to a counselling service in a university might reflect that to the institution as a whole:

A counsellor working in a university gave an account of a session with a student client she was working with. The student was leaving the university at the end of term and had said, 'I'm worried that there are only four more lessons – I mean sessions – before we have to finish – I don't know whether I'll have dealt with everything by then . . .' The counsellor was very struck by this slip of the tongue; she knew that the student client was repeating the year because she had not been able to set herself realistic deadlines in the previous academic year. This in turn reflected her anxiety about leaving the university and entering the world of work.

In this case the client was apparently thinking of the university counselling service as a sort of extension of the academic courses, which in turn were something to be got through as painlessly as possible – her previous experiences of education had not been happy ones. The question of how the counsellor is seen by the client in relation to their role in the institution needs to be thought about in supervision, since it relates to the kind of interventions that might make an impact on the client.

Enactments and acting out: pressure on therapists

We have already thought about some of the pressures that clients coming to counselling services put on their counsellors, and how they can feel manipulated into acting out of role. Supervisors can help think through the implications of what has happened and how this can be used in future work.

A supervisee working in a youth counselling service talked of a young client, with a history of self harm, who came into the session with a bandaged arm. This situation was addressed by the counsellor in the session, although the client was unwilling to let her know very much about what was going on.

After the session the counsellor was about to leave the building and go home when she saw that the client was still in reception, and upset as the cut on her arm had started bleeding again. No one else was around. The counsellor assessed the situation – something needed to be done as the bandage clearly wasn't adequate. However she didn't feel the situation was serious enough to call an ambulance. In the end she found the first-aid kit, took the client into the women's cloakroom and put on a new bandage, with instructions to get it looked at by her GP.

When we talked about the situation, neither of us was in any doubt that she had done the best thing under the circumstances. But she needed to process the kind of pressure she had been put under;

having to touch the client had gone against her training, making her feel unbounded, and there was something slightly sordid about having to use the toilets for this purpose. She thought this was perhaps connected with a very intimate, almost sexual feeling about the bandaging. When she thought about it, she felt quite angry with the client for putting her in this position.

This led on to a discussion about how this episode might be taken up with the client, in terms of her longing for my supervisee to care for her in a different way, but also in terms of the more destructive aspects – it was a challenge to the boundaries of the counselling. My supervisee later made very good use of the event to consider these and related issues with the client. Thinking more practically, we also wondered about aspects of the organisation and its procedures and whether there might be someone else who could potentially carry out a more practical role in such circumstances.

Summary and conclusions

In this chapter we have thought about the extra dimension involved in supervising those working in institutions of various kinds. Institutions generate anxiety, which may relate to the influence of group processes and the way in which the dynamics of the primary task are played out in this setting. We consider this in the light of psychoanalytic and systems theory. Good supervision can help the therapist manage these influences and allow them to focus on the client and it may also help them to reconsider procedures in a way which is helpful to their colleagues as well as in their own work. The chapter ends with some thoughts about some of the practical implications of supervising those working in institutions.

Some concluding points about working in institutions are highlighted below:

- Those supervising in or for institutions have to accept that many organisations will have an ambivalent view of the value of the therapeutic work which they are supervising. This is particularly true where the primary task of the organisation is not therapeutic. In other organisations an apparent idealisation of psychodynamic work is counteracted by scarcities of resources and other obstacles, reflecting the difficulties of thinking about the emotional and psychological distress that is the subject matter of counselling and psychotherapy.

- Partly because of these dynamics, therapists working in institutions have to guard against being overwhelmed by the weight of the organisation's expectations and the accompanying anxiety.

- Part of the function of supervision under these circumstances is to help the supervisee think realistically about their interaction with the organisation; they have to help them find a path between being feeling overwhelmed by the pressure of work or alternatively becoming detached as a defence against the anxiety generated within the institution.

- Just as their supervisees will find that their boundaries are attacked at times, so supervisors have to think about their own boundaries. Thinking about organisational dynamics in supervision might be appropriate in the role of supervisor, and will allow the supervisee to take up the role of providing a psychodynamic input to difficult situations.

- However, the supervisor needs to be aware of their own role and consider where to draw the line – getting involved in informal consultation to the organisation, through the medium of the supervisee, could be taking a step too far. Thinking about where to draw the line involves a constant attention to roles and functions as well as other idiosyncratic factors.

8

WORKING WITH DIFFERENCE

Introduction

This chapter considers a further aspect of the context of supervision, that of differences between the patient, therapist and supervisor. We have seen that different points of view are bound to emerge in the process of supervision, since a major part of the supervisor's role is to stand back and provide an alternative perspective on events unfolding in the counselling or therapy. These perspectives have their roots in differences in levels of experience, in views of the function of counselling or therapy, in ideas about what the events in the consulting room mean, as well as in the particular dynamics of the individual relationship. We might welcome the stimulus and challenge on one level but it can also be painful, because to acknowledge any difference means acknowledging the existence of qualities in the other that we lack ourselves.

This chapter, however, will consider the impact of other, more personal and in some ways more obvious differences – colour and race, and gender come to mind immediately. These characteristics are an important part of our identity, having an enormous influence on how we see others and ourselves, and how we are seen in turn. It is in the nature of such differences that we will all consider different areas – maybe age, disability, sexual orientation or social class – to be more or less significant. This may partly depend on whether the type of difference allows us to position ourselves as in a dominant or majority position, or as on the margins of a group or society in general. Such differences, and the influence they have on the dynamics of our inner worlds, can get in the way of the task of supervision if they cannot be acknowledged and worked with.

Perspectives on difference

A criticism often levelled by those coming from other theoretical orientations is that a psychoanalytic approach, in focussing primarily on the internal world of the patient, does not allow for a proper weight to be given to the effect of external circumstances, including socio-cultural and economic factors, and their relation to personal characteristics, physical and otherwise. There is, in addition, the idea that psychoanalysis because of its origins is bound to take a Eurocentric perspective, and is inherently imbued with a white, middle class and indeed masculine standpoint.

Counselling trainings and writings have more frequently taken a lead in considering the topic of difference; although, as Helen Morgan (2007) writes, sometimes they take up the stance of thinking more in terms of culture (moving to a more anthropological way of seeing things) and less about the impact of the situation on the inner world of the individual (p. 190). We have seen that this tension between the inner world and its interaction with external reality is a constant theme in supervision.

Writers vary in the different importance they give to the role of knowledge of cultural practices when working cross-culturally. Paul Gordon (1996) warns against overvaluing a relatively superficial knowledge of a culture at the expense of finding out what membership means for the individual. Alessandra Lemma (1999), writing of her experience of working in Bangladesh, identifies basic cultural differences to do with the importance of the family as opposed to the individual, as well as other circumstances which suggest that in some circumstances a modification of a more traditional psychoanalytic frame and technique is needed. However, both emphasise the need for practitioners to be curious and sensitive to individual cultural experience.

The difficulties related to difference often arise at a much more basic level, that of the immediate impact we have on each other. Colour, age and gender are the characteristics we notice straightaway when we encounter another person, and in themselves they are unalterable, although of course our perceptions of them may change. These and other differences contribute to Bion's 'emotional storm', a feature of any new encounter (op. cit., Chapter 2). In addition, colour, because it can indicate membership of an ethnic minority group, is a difference which has historically been associated with power imbalances, part of the legacy of Britain's colonial past. As with other dimensions of difference the issues involved are complex and engender a great deal of pain, demor-alisation and anger, particularly for members of ethnic minorities, as well as an often counterproductive guilt on the part of white therapists.

Counsellors and psychotherapists often feel very diffident about raising questions of difference in therapy sessions; there can be a retreat into a concrete, magical way of thinking where naming a phenomenon is seen as making matters worse. There are also times when more general discussion of the subject can take on a criti-cal tone dominated by superego influences; none of us want to be thought overtly racist or sexist, but fear of this can censor our think-ing, and result in a tendency to focus on any evidence that it exists in others. In practice it can be difficult to understand and articu-late the many different ways in which individual, often externally perceived, characteristics – colour and other characteristics of ethnic groups, age and gender for example – affect our experience and the way we react to others and they to us. Even before the first meet-ing these stereotypes are in our minds; as Jafar Kareem (1988, p. 63) writes, 'Transference and countertransference do not wait to happen in the consulting room. Transference has already taken place before the treatment has started.'

I found myself thinking that if I had written this book 30 years ago, a discussion of gender issues would probably have taken centre stage. This brings up one of the fundamental problems in thinking about difference, that when discussing this subject it is very easy to minimise the importance of any individual difference by switch-ing the focus and bringing in other areas that need discussion. In some cases similar dynamics operate as for racial and gender differ-ences; sometimes, where we are confronted with the effects of illness, injury or aging, the emphasis may be more on loss and the need to deny this.

Part of the work of supervision and therapy is to monitor the way we perceive and react to others, whatever our own background. Richard Tan (1993, p. 43), writing on the unconscious dynamics of racism, says that where this is disavowed, there will always be a 'feeling of uncertainty and ambivalence about another of a different race'. He goes on:

> ... it is vital that psychoanalytic psychotherapists have the abil-ity to examine their own unconscious feelings and phantasies about racial difference, so as to be less influenced by their own omnipotence, and in turn, by that of the patient. I believe this to

be the first obstacle for us to be aware of before any growth can begin to germinate, especially when therapist and patient are from different racial groupings.

It is painful to have to confront our own assumptions and prejudices, but it is part of the process we have to engage with all the time, in the service of processing our own countertransference. Part of the difficulty is that we are dealing with aspects of our identity that cannot be changed, and sometimes this realisation is very painful; it touches on our narcissism, and brings home to us our limitations.

A further difficulty might be that we seem to find it easier to think of ourselves as the victims of circumstances than acknowledge the power we have to inflict pain on others, however unwittingly. This might account for the fact that discussions focusing on one difference often get sidetracked by those who want to draw a parallel with another dimension of difference; any difference has the possibility of being used for the function of projecting undesirable qualities onto other individuals or groups.

In clinical settings, the strength of the feelings engendered by some kinds of differences and the assumptions that are linked to them can take us by surprise.

An example comes to mind, of a black client I saw many years ago in a student counselling setting, in connection with his need to think about a violent relationship with his female partner, also black, but from a different culture. When I addressed the issue of what it might mean to be coming to see a white counsellor he was very keen to point out that it was my gender that was the real difficulty – he assumed that, as a woman, I would be intolerant of his difficulty. I initially took this at face value, but we later came to understand that there was in fact an enormous shame at having to talk to a white woman; in the transference I represented various critical and cruel white authority figures in his background who had made him feel ashamed and ignorant. This compounded his identification of me with his partner and made the humiliation of the therapeutic situation almost unbearable.

I should say here that, in common with other writers on the subject of race and ethnicity (see, e.g., Davids (2003); Dalal (2002)) I use the terms 'black' and 'white' when exploring interactions where race/ethnic group is an important dimension of difference which has become significant. In using these terms I recognise that race is an empty category (see below) in terms of objective criteria.

However I use them to draw attention to the impact of perceived differences between members of different ethnic groups.

A further function of supervision, then, is to help our supervisees think about how they are seen by their patient or clients; this is inevitably a complex mixture of 'real life' characteristics to do with our ethnicity, age, gender, class and so on, and the way in which these characteristics evoke a particular transference reaction in our patients. Supervisees have to be encouraged to think about this and to bear the often difficult countertransference feelings engendered by the assumptions being made about them. This will be easier if they have a realistic sense of themselves and are aware of the way they appear to others as well as their own more problematic characteristics and tendencies.

Theories and examples relating to colour and race differences

Michael Rustin (1991) has described race as an 'empty category', in that there are only very small relatively superficial differences between the races, to do with external appearances (pp. 57–59). This, as he points out, does not prevent such characteristics from being used to create ways of identifying and discriminating against people who are defined as coming from a particular racial group – rather, it makes the process easier. In common with a number of writers (see, e.g., Tan (op. cit.) and Timimi (1996)) he considers the mechanisms of projection and projective identification to be important processes by which particular (unwanted or disavowed) qualities are linked with a representative of particular ethnic groups.

Fakhry Davids has put forward the idea that these mechanisms are organised into a psychic structure which he terms an internal racist organisation, a feature which he considers to be universal. It is activated as a way of defending against uncertainty. He gives an example of this process in his (2003b) account of a situation in which a white patient, extremely ill and anxious at the commencement of therapy, responded to an interpretation by getting violently angry. This was experienced in the countertransference as a racist attack, and the truth of this was confirmed in a subsequent session, when the patient voiced his concern that his analyst would not be able to understand his difficulties, since he clearly came from another culture. To avoid facing his own disorientation and dependency, he had pushed it into his analyst, using racial and colour differences to make him the disadvantaged one.

Farhad Dalal (2002) writes on other perspectives (historical, group analytic and psychoanalytic among others) that can be brought to bear on the study of racism and racialised thinking. His account highlights the importance of power differentials in reinforcing the use of difference as well as the group processes that contribute towards a racist society. He (op. cit., p. 7) writes, when introducing his work:

> difference is not the cause of hatred, rather particular differences are called forth by the vicissitudes of power relations in order to organise hatred (and other emotions) in order to achieve particular ends. These mechanisms work by lending the differences and the required hatreds an air of naturalness and so legitimises them. One such difference is that of race, which because of its fragility relies on the notion of colour. And finally, it is shown that the structures of society are reflected in the structures of the psyche, and if the first of these is colour coded, then so will be the second.

Morgan (1998), who has written extensively about racism in the consulting room, makes the point that it is differences in colour, not culture or any other feature that might coincide with skin colour, that initially arouse our most primitive anxieties. She considers that this is important, not only because thoughts about difference and the unfamiliar are difficult to process but because of power differentials between people of different colours that are inevitably embedded in the minds of all of us when we meet. She writes, 'Because we work in an essentially white profession within a society where white holds power, the white therapist can go through life avoiding this matter altogether, assuming it to be a problem for our black colleagues.'

Historically, psychoanalytic and psychoanalytic psychotherapy circles have been dominated by the white majority; this is less true for those working in the counselling profession. In both therapy and supervision the issue of colour and race has sometimes been circumvented by making the assumption that, in our inner worlds, we are all the same. In a recent (2007) paper on race and supervision, Morgan quotes Margaret James-Franklin's research on the experience of black psychoanalytic psychotherapists in training. It seems that they often found they could only survive the training process by putting aside their 'blackness'; their trainers tended to take a colour-blind position and this meant that they were not able to help with interpretation of some aspects of the transference, relating to colour. As Morgan points out, when it comes to the issue of colour and race white supervisors and therapists need to learn from black colleagues and supervisees. I have found that black supervisees are generally more likely to be able to raise the subject of race with their clients. But we also have to guard against putting them in a special position, particularly in groups where they are the only black member, of being expected to represent an ethnic minority point of view.

As supervisors, we need to be alert to the dynamics of racial difference and racism, since these may result in black supervisees and patients being disadvantaged. This is partly because of the strength of the projective processes described above, as well as their incorporation into a psychic organisation that may use racism defensively. But in addition, as Aileen Alleyne (2005) points out, oppression can be internalised, resulting in tendencies to sabotage one's own work in various ways. She is writing about relations in the workplace but it is equally applicable in other situations. This case illustrates this point:

A black male supervisee, Matthew, was working with a white client, also male, who came to a counselling service because of difficulties at work and in making friends. Initially the client had a tendency to idealise his counsellor, asking his advice and treating him as an expert, particularly in the matter of relationships. He seemed to want to give this relationship a social flavour, complimenting Matthew on his clothes and appearance.

In supervision Matthew's (white) supervisor urged him to take up the matter of these personal remarks, which Matthew, being at the beginning of his counselling career, found difficult to deal with. He became hesitant in his dealings with the client, who reacted by making more and more unbounded remarks, finally going into a grotesque imitation of a black man talking in dialect, while still apparently professing his admiration. Matthew was shocked into silence.

Matthew felt powerless and discouraged; the client was difficult and contemptuous, but he also felt unsupported in supervision. In fact he felt pinioned between these two white people. As for his supervisor, he thought she could have no idea what it felt like being mocked like this, and he felt exposed at having to recount the episode in supervision.

He was late for the next session with the client, who had never been a regular attendee but used this as an excuse to give up the counselling.

In this example we can see that the client used a racist attack to undermine the work, perhaps in this case out of envy (Matthew was seen as being more successful in all sorts of ways.) Matthew acted out his feelings of being demoralised by being late, the client having successfully got rid of his own feelings of incompetence by evacuating them into Matthew. This seems to be an illustration of Frank Lowe's (2008) account of the way in which what he terms 'Colonial object relations' can develop. The white client attempted to control his counsellor and managed to succeed in disabling him, partly because Matthew found himself unwittingly identifying with the client's racist caricature of a black man.

When the matter was discussed in supervision, the supervisor realised that she could have been more helpful to Matthew. She could have taken more trouble to explore the nature of the inter-actions in the sessions and what it meant to Matthew as a black counsellor. Also, because he had seemed compliant, in terms of apparently recognising the need to address the matter, she had not elaborated sufficiently on the ways in which he might take up mat-ters with the client. She had not appreciated the extent to which his frustration with supervision had been masked by his apparent equanimity.

White liberals, and the psychotherapy profession generally, would naturally repudiate racism in its most violent, obvious forms. What can happen, however, is that thoughts that we might have about members of ethnic minorities can be driven underground; we suppress them or deny them because of our guilt and shame about having such thoughts and because of the way white people have treated black people in the past. This means that differences in colour get overlaid with various assumptions and prejudices, on both sides.

The following example shows the power of a largely unconscious fear that initially affected a white therapist's work with a black female patient:

In her peer supervision group, Esther presented a session with a black (Asian) female patient that she was seeing three times a week, in connec-tion with serious difficulties in forming relationships. The patient missed many sessions, and when this happened Esther would experience a very strong emotional reaction – anger combined with a real sense of loss and disappointment. (She thought of this as a countertransference reaction, associated with her patient's early experiences, which were of an incon-sistent maternal object.) She was always relieved when the patient did turn up, usually giving very 'good' reasons for her absence, to do with external circumstances.

The latest absence concerned the patient's need to accompany her mother, a woman previously described as being in robust health, to the GP for what sounded like a routine appointment. The patient had delivered this information triumphantly. Esther's concern was that after an initial feeling of irritation, she had felt completely tongue tied. She had said something rather half hearted about her relationship with her mother and then the patient moved to other matters.

Esther told her colleagues that she felt rather shamed by her failure to take up the matter of absence, particularly as it was the latest in a long line and the therapy was really in jeopardy. Two of the group were inclined to be dismissive – they could not see quite what the difficulty was. The fourth member of the group, who was himself a member of an ethnic minority, was able to take a different perspective. He thought that racial issues might come into this interaction, and that Esther's failure to challenge the missed sessions was related to a somewhat exaggerated fear of offending or misunderstanding the patient. Was there an assumption that a black patient should not be challenged? If so, this sounded patronising.

Esther thought about the session and said that she had had several thoughts about the reason given for the absence which she had not wanted to voice at the time, since they remained in a raw, unprocessed state. She had suppressed a thought about the mother's inability to get herself to the GP – the thought went through her mind that she had surely been in the country long enough to be able to manage this! Was her daughter at her beck and call? She had then felt ashamed of this thought because of the way the subject of her patient's ethnicity (and related immigrant status) was powerfully linked in her mind to her own anger about the missed session. Then she thought that perhaps she was envious of this woman's relationship with her mother – they were close, in a way she initially thought she did not quite understand, unlike a cold white family. This of course was going to the opposite extreme and idealising the patient and her family setup – and Esther had plenty of reported information which showed this was an unrealistic view.

The effect of these thoughts had been to throw her into confusion. She had also felt annoyed – and reproached – by the triumph in her patient's voice, which she had initially taken to be saying, 'you see – we do things better than you'. This perception was of course related to her own superego anxieties as well as to the patient's way of speaking.

The effect of these commonplace, but to Esther, disturbing, ideas was to paralyse her in the session, so that she could not see the material *in terms of the attack on the therapy. As a result, the patient, already disadvantaged in all sorts of ways, was in danger of getting a less rigorous therapy and perhaps leaving prematurely because the therapist had allowed herself to become disabled and immobilised by her thoughts about the racial difference.*

In supervision, we need to be free to explore these initially unacceptable thoughts, or there is a danger that the fear of being thought racist (or prejudiced in other ways) will paralyse our thinking. We also need to look out for the various ways in which racial difference is being used in the transference. Sometimes there is an apparent idealisation of white culture, which adds to existing dynamics to do with power differentials between therapist and patient.

Mary brought to supervision a young Asian woman, Parvati, whom she was seeing at the university counselling service. Her client complained of the pressures her mother was putting on her to look after her brother's new baby, to the detriment of her studies (it was a joint household so it was apparently hard to avoid this task). She felt very angry with her mother and by extension the baby; the violence of her feelings disconcerted her, which was why she had come to counselling. There was a furious outpouring of feelings about the traditional, old-fashioned views that her parents held, and their doubts about the value of a university education for a woman. Her mother was so limited in her outlook, had no idea of what she was trying to achieve, by getting a degree. She was being made to be an unpaid childminder. Mary felt under a lot of pressure to agree that this was quite unreasonable.

In supervision, Mary said that to begin with she had been concerned about the baby but it had soon been established that Parvati was very fond of the baby and actually would never harm her. The supervisor said that the issue seemed to be that Mary was being invited to identify with the client, to be an ally in Parvati's conflict with her parents. In one sense she was being set up as an idealised white liberal parent, or an ally, but at the same time being invited to take up a potentially culturally insensitive view of the situation.

When Mary said something to Parvati about the nature of the role she was being assigned, the fragility of this idealisation struck home; it was clear that Parvati was disconcerted and felt unsupported by her counsellor. But this state of mind did allow her to realise that her anger was a more general phenomenon, not only with her parents but also with others in authority. There was also a realisation that she was quite envious of her sister-in-law for having had this baby, as well as wanting to be involved in her care. The following session, she told Mary that she'd had a conversation with her mother that seemed to be making a difference.

In the above example it could be argued that an adolescent conflict had become associated in the client's mind with a cultural characteristic; the unravelling of these different strands was part of the work of supervision.

There can be a danger that when supervising work across cultural lines we get over concerned with one difference and fail to recognise other differences, which later become blindingly obvious. Renos Papadopoulos (2002), writing about working with refugee families, considers the way in which those working in the field can get overwhelmed by the idea of the traumas which their clients have suffered, and assume that special knowledge and techniques are needed. He quotes an example of supervising the case of a refugee child, Zahra, whose difficulties were assumed to be solely related to the aspects of her history that connected with her refugee status and the war in her country of origin. He was able to help those involved to see that in fact this child had suffered multiple losses, in terms of parents dying and changes in caretaking arrangements and that it was the effect of these on her present situation that were the prime consideration (op. cit., pp. 163–167).

Gender and sexuality

We have seen that psychoanalytic theories, particularly those using post-Kleinian ideas about splitting and projective identification, can help us think about racial difference and racism. When it come to thinking about sexual difference the picture is more complicated, partly because of the multiplicity of ways in which sexual development and identity has been conceptualised by the psychoanalytic movement (for a comprehensive description of the different strands of thought over time see, e.g., Stephen Frosh's (1997) chapter on psychoanalytic agendas).

Gender as well as colour is a difference that we cannot fail to notice consciously as soon as we meet someone – but it also generates assumptions and reactions at a deeper level, related to our emotional and sexual development. These dynamics will be present in therapy sessions and in supervision, whether in the form of Oedipal rivalries, eroticised transferences or perceived – or misperceived – power imbalances.

Earlier in the chapter I outlined the idea of internalised oppressors in connection with race and colour issues. The same idea has been applied to women in relation to their views of men; as Jane Temperley wrote in her (1984) paper, 'Our own worst enemies', women can at times react to aggression and competition, seeing them as male attributes. She considers ways in which women may undermine their own progress in employment and other areas; one of these is based on an identification with a denigrated maternal object and a corresponding idealisation of male figures and their qualities. She also considers that women can gain a certain satisfaction in being subordinate, a victim occupying the moral high ground (pp. 27–31). The following example illustrates something of this underlying dynamic:

> June was a trainee psychotherapist working with a male patient on an intensive basis. Her supervisor was also male and from the start it seemed as if he identified with the patient and his culture – they both came from the same distant part of the country, and had similar backgrounds, an area of which June had no knowledge. The patient was finding the start of therapy difficult to manage. He was very anxious, and would show this by missing sessions and being late and often uncommunicative when he did attend. June had worked with male patients before but felt there was something quite unknowable about this man. She felt alienated and excluded. As a result she found it very hard to challenge him, and when she did she got a very negative response. She retreated into a cautious and rather passive state of mind, although actually she felt very frustrated. This also seemed to be true of the supervisor, who was impatient, and the patient, who just seemed stuck.
>
> When they reviewed the work, the supervisor commented on the hopelessness of the case and wondered whether she could find an alternative, 'better' patient. It was clear he also thought June could be much more proactive. June found it hard not to feel identified with this unsatisfactory patient; they were both a disappointment to her supervisor. She knew that some of her feelings related to the powerful way in which the patient was projecting his anxiety and hopelessness into her. But in her more regressed moments she also found it hard not to see both the supervisor and patient as being allied against her, as an incompetent woman, from a position of male solidarity and superiority. She was on the way towards nurturing a sense of grievance.

She only realised how identified she had become with this hopeless image when one day, to her surprise, she confronted her supervisor after what she thought was a particularly harsh comment. She was equally surprised to find that he took her seriously and a much more collegiate, helpful dynamic developed. She later realised that her passivity had probably been counterproductive and quite irritating, possibly also to the patient who needed a more active containment.

In this case we can see that there are a number of contributing factors to the situation – the fact that it takes place in the context of a training, where there are greater power and experience differentials, idiosyncratic character traits as well as the male–female divide. As supervisors, we can help by being aware of these dynamics, and we also have to recognise that for many reasons not all supervisees are equally robust. This is not to suggest we should always make allowances:

A supervisee training in a community counselling service said that she only wanted to see women clients – she had had abusive experiences of men at earlier points in her life. The supervisor thought abut this; she was concerned about the supervisee becoming a 'special case', limiting her development as a counsellor, and as the service provided for both men and women, she felt this was not a reasonable position in the long run. In analytic terms, she was also concerned about the implication that abuse and aggression were located solely in men; she could see that the supervisee was employing an excessive degree of projective identification in her thinking on the subject. After some discussion, they compromised. The supervisee agreed that she needed to think about this matter and decided to increase the number of her therapy sessions to explore this issue and the supervisor agreed that the first client could be a woman, and then they would review the position. When the matter was explored in more detail, it seemed that a lot of the anxiety was about beginning the work with clients, but had focussed on gender differences as a way of managing this anxiety.

This vignette illustrates something of the tension between holding in mind the 'real life' differences that we have been considering in this chapter, while continuing to think about how they might be perceived or linked with other characteristics. Sometimes there is an attempt to eliminate problems connected with difference by trying to select counsellors for clients on the basis of perceived similarities.

It is common in charitable agencies working in specific areas to find that volunteer and some professional counsellors are expected to have had experience of the issues being worked with. The rationale seems to be to do with the need for empathy; that only those who have suffered in the same way can really understand what it is like to be affected by these issues, particularly if they have not had a professional training. In addition, the clients are often, perhaps rightly, assumed to prefer to work with someone who is the same in some important respect; this is particularly true of woman who have been victimised in some way, or clients who have suffered a particular type of loss.

The problem with this stance is that it privileges a rather concrete level of identification, and ignores the role of the imagination in empathising; also, as experienced counsellors, therapists and supervisors, we know that in the transference we can be seen in many different guises, whatever our colour or gender, and that it is not helpful to limit these by implicitly disclosing personal information.

This question of the ability to be flexible in countertransference responses is one that Joy Schaverien (2003) considers in relation to working with the erotic transference in supervision; part of her paper considers the way that preconceptions about the sexual orientation of the therapist can influence the course of therapy and prevent exploration of sexual issues (pp. 179–182). This can be disconcerting, particularly for inexperienced counsellors and therapists, who may be concerned that these feelings are going to spill over into the rest of their life; they do not have a sense of how strong the countertransference can be. In addition they may not have had the opportunity to explore fully aspects of their own sexuality in therapy; they may be shocked to experience feelings which apparently run counter to their own sexual orientation.

Tina was working with Natalia, a young woman who had come to the counselling service because an early experience of being sexually abused by an older cousin had begun to trouble her. As the work went on, Tina was shocked to find herself experiencing very strong sexual feelings while being in the room with Natalia. As someone who has always thought of herself as solidly heterosexual, this was disconcerting.

She kept these feelings to herself but eventually felt she had to tell her supervisor. Going into the situation in more detail allowed her to see that the shame she felt was partly related to the sense of something forbidden being re-enacted, in the counselling room; that it has been arousing but at the same time a forbidden secret experience which made her feel

*very guilty. Natalia has not been able to talk about the guilty plea-
sure involved in this experience, but it made sense to Tina, in terms of
Natalia's continual anxiety as to whether people outside the room could
hear what they were talking about – if there were noises outside, she
jumped. In her mind, the experience of being in the room with just one
other person, the counsellor, had been linked to her experience of being
with her brother, and had recreated some of the same feelings, which were
then experienced by Tina.*

At this point Tina also had some thinking to do on her own behalf;
although this was not on her agenda for supervision, she realised she
needed to think about her own feelings in the session; why had she
been so shocked – did this imply that there was a part of her that
she did not know about or understand? It might be equally disconcerting for homosexual therapists to discover erotic feelings about
opposite-sex clients, but as the above example shows, supervisors
need to cultivate an atmosphere where issues of sexual attraction
can be explored, in the service of understanding the material than the
client brings to the sessions. In this context it has to be acknowledged
that traditional ways of conceptualising homosexuality on the part
of the psychoanalytic profession, seeing it in terms of a developmental failure, or a perversion, have not made it easier for this issue
to be discussed in supervision (for a thoughtful examination of this
subject, see the recent paper by Sidney Phillips (2003)).

Age differences

One difference which is considered relatively infrequently, in terms
of its impact on therapy and supervision, is that of age. Perhaps part
of the reason is that, in contrast to some other more innate differences, there might be an assumption that we know more about this
subject, since we have all had an experience of being young and we
might hope to know something about getting older. But people's
experience and expectations of these different stages in life, and their
ability to think about the losses involved in getting older, are very
different. This might make it harder, not easier, to tolerate as a point
of difference. The same projective processes that are apt to come into
work with those of a different ethnic group can come into and interfere with therapy and supervision. Paul Terry (op. cit., pp. 113–122),
writing about these projective processes, considers ageist attitudes
and behaviours in the context of working with the elderly, and

the way in which there can be a constant mutual projection and re-introjection of feelings of helplessness and fears of dependency and death.

These dynamics are potentially there, perhaps in a less powerful form, in therapy and supervision. There can be a tendency to feel that older clients are somehow more fragile mentally as well as physically, and should not be confronted with the reality of their impending death. An interpretation can feel like an attack in these circumstances, as though the client has not got the ability to think symbolically. Of course in this situation it is the counsellor who may be protecting themselves from the need to think, among other things, about their own fears of aging and associated disability, as well as the sadism involved in projecting these feelings into their client.

Age differences can also come into supervision more directly; younger supervisees may for various reasons feel scornful of older supervisors while supervisors may have to think about their envy of those with more working years ahead of them. These dynamics are perhaps more likely to arise when the supervisee is older than the supervisor; some supervisees can find this a humiliating situation and become more obstreperous or envious as a result.

Disability

With disability as with age, it is very often our need to disavow our experience, rather than a lack of experience, that complicates matters:

> Zoë, a volunteer counsellor working in a hospice, brought her client to supervision; this was a woman 20 years older than Zoë who was faced with a life-threatening illness. At first Zoë had been full of admiration for the way her patient was managing this situation, but she was shocked to find herself getting increasingly irritated. Her supervisor noted that, interestingly, this irritation increased at the point when it seemed as if her patient would after all live a little longer, and was beginning to think of leaving counselling. It was compounded when the supervisor took a week off with the flu.
>
> When they thought about this together, Zoë said that it had been hard to work with this client – her own mother had died from the illness that this client was suffering from. Zoë envied her client's family who would have her around for a little longer. On the other hand, the supervisor

being away had reminded her of what it felt like to be abandoned when somebody dies, when you feel too young and vulnerable to manage by yourself. In addition, she had found herself getting preoccupied with her own health, over identifying with the client as an unconscious way of trying to feel more empathetic.

In this case we can see that both similarity and difference are involved in the dynamics. Zoë expected to feel sympathetic and thought that she knew something of the issues involved. When her own mother had died, she had gained some satisfaction from being supportive and helpful, but of course in other unacknowledged ways there was some guilt involved, possibly just because she had realised how happy she was to be alive. Becoming involved in working with those suffering from a terminal illness was, in her eyes, a way of making up for this. Until she thought about it in supervision, she had not realised how important it was for her to be the healthy one.

Julia Segal (1996) in her consideration of problems of working with disabled clients highlights the importance of counsellors and therapists considering their own phantasies about what it might mean to be disabled. When she investigated this subject, she found that very often there were unduly pessimistic views about the quality of life that could be achieved, with a tendency to idealise or denigrate the disabled, as well as fear of their envy. She (p. 158) also noted that contrary to her expectations, envy of the able bodied was not necessarily a significant dynamic with clients who were physically ill, or even those with life-threatening or limiting illnesses. She found it more likely to arise with those who were suffering from a mental illness.

Sometimes it is difficult to separate out different aspects of disability:

Gavin was working with Sally, a wheelchair user all her life. She was finding her university course very difficult, and was constantly wanting Gavin to act as an advocate for her in getting extra time for assignments and other special arrangements. Initially the need for this was, of course, accepted. As time went on however, it seemed as though nothing could ever be completed; there were always prosaic, practical reasons why things went wrong. When this happened she would place more demands on Gavin, changing appointment times, and sometimes getting very anxious, almost on the edge of a breakdown. This was very worrying to Gavin, who felt quite paralysed, as well as concerned.

When he had a chance to think about it in supervision, he realised that he had focussed on her physical disability and what it prevented her from achieving. It was very hard for him to consider the possibility that it might be emotional or mental difficulties, related perhaps to the particular circumstances of her upbringing, that prevented her from participating in the course. This was in part because Sally herself found it impossible to face these issues, relating everything back to her physical difficulties, which she felt entitled her to unlimited special treatment. Beginning to think with her about this issue felt like adding insult to injury.

The last example relates to differences we have considered already as well as another difference – that of assumed personal experience – and shows the complexity of the differences that might inhibit discussion in supervision:

Paul brought his client, Ruth, to a group consisting of the supervisor and two others, Charlotte and Devika. His fellow supervisees, as well as the supervisor, were women in their fifties, while he was much younger. Paul was working very sensitively with Ruth, who had come to counselling because of depression relating to a history of miscarriage, and a recent stillbirth. Ruth's situation had aroused a great deal of empathy and interest within the group; there was a shared excitement in the fact that Ruth had recently announced she was pregnant. It was clear that everyone identified with her hopes that this time, a healthy baby would be born.

On one occasion supervision had to be cancelled and the supervisor arranged to speak with the supervisees individually by telephone. In Paul's case, he began by saying that he wanted to speak about a dream that he had had the previous week. The dream was that he and his client were lying in bed together, and there was a baby there that had been created between them. But there was also an older woman there – in the dream he wasn't sure why she was there and he thought that she might interfere with or otherwise harm this very precious baby. The supervisor took this up, quite humorously, as a reference to supervision and whether the scrutiny involved might spoil things between the client and the supervisee. Paul was ready to acknowledge that this was a plausible explanation. But then he said 'I'm glad I have had the opportunity to speak about this with you alone . . . you see I was concerned about telling it in the group. I have the idea that you do have children, but I know that the others haven't. It feels awkward and I suppose I am worried about stirring up envy – not just because of the work with R, which is so interesting, but also because in real life I have children and they don't.'

The supervisor's response was that she appreciated his sensitivity but she wanted to encourage him to share the dream next time the group met. She thought his fellow supervisees were robust and would have something useful to contribute on the subject. This turned out to be the case.

Paul told the others of his dream and the resulting discussion was a very rich mixture of thoughts and associations. There was some acknowledgement that the others would also have liked to work with this client. Charlotte said that she thought Paul felt under pressure – there were effectively three mothers all keeping a close eye on what the two of them were up to, in the counselling; she thought this must be very inhibiting. The supervisor then wondered about Ruth's partner – he hadn't come into the picture much and perhaps there was a shared phantasy that Paul was the real partner. At this point Devika remarked that Paul and Ruth were white but Ruth's partner in real life was black; she wondered whether Ruth was beginning to have some mixed feelings about her black partner, and was beginning to feel indentified with, and attracted to, Paul. Devika, looking at things from her own perspective as a member of an ethnic minority, drew the group's attention to something that they might not have felt able to articulate, the idea that Ruth, at an unconscious level, might think of her partner as inferior because he was a member of an ethnic minority group. This was a painful idea for the group to consider, for various reasons, and they did not dwell on it for long. But it did seem to add weight to the idea of an idealised and somewhat eroticised transference, reflected in the dream, which in turn represented an aspect of the countertransference that had not come to light until then.

Summary and conclusions

In this chapter we have considered aspects of difference and the challenges they pose in supervision. In particular I have focussed on the issues that are likely to arise when there are differences to do with ethnicity and colour. Such differences can be used to reinforce power differentials operating in the external world and inevitably affect our perceptions of ourselves in relation to others. This subject is one where polarised thinking – idealisation and denigration – as well as projection and projective identification – are likely to predominate. Because of the strength of the feelings generated, supervisees can become anxious and inhibited in their thinking and in thinking about these issues with their patients and in supervision.

For similar reasons differences such as gender and sexual orientation are also likely to activate strong feelings and may also be difficult to acknowledge if therapists have not been able to think about their own sexuality and their prejudices. In addition, aspects of sexual orientation have always been the subject of controversy in psychoanalytic circles. Disability and aging are subjects that bring up issues to do with loss and mourning and it can be very difficult for therapists to stay with these feelings when working with patients.

Some points in conclusion:

- We have seen that differences can be used in various ways, perhaps most commonly to evacuate qualities or attributes that cause anxiety into other people or groups of people, so that the others can be hated or despised. When difference is linked to power differentials this type of projective process becomes very powerful.

- Working with any difference in supervision is complex because it involves acknowledging our own prejudices about other groups or individuals, in a way that may seem counterintuitive in a cultural climate where voicing these thoughts seems to go against notions of political correctness as well as tactfulness.

- In addition to thinking about our thoughts about others, there is the painfulness of acknowledging how we might be seen by others, because of our personal characteristics. Our own characteristics inevitably interact with the patients' thoughts and phantasies and contribute to the transference. This brings up the subject of the negative transference, and enabling our supervisees to bear this and think about it is a very important task of supervision.

- We need to be able to create a space in supervision where these dynamics can be explored, if our supervisees are to be able to contain their anxieties and think about their meaning when working with patients.

CHALLENGES AND DILEMMAS IN SUPERVISION

Introduction

This chapter considers situations that present a particular challenge to the supervisor. Crises or difficulties can have their origins in any part of the supervisory triangle. We have seen that difficulties in the therapeutic relationship can be reflected in the supervisory relationship. But the reverse is also true; if supervisees do not feel supported and contained in the supervision, their patients can suffer. This chapter will also consider further the subject of the supervisor's role in terms of thinking about containment of anxiety in institutions. Sometimes, these situations call for the supervisor to focus more on the monitoring and managerial function of supervision, as well as an educational or supportive role.

Many of the examples in this book have dealt with situations where there has been pressure from the client or patient to pull the therapist out of role. For example, in Chapter 7 I gave the instance of the supervisee who found herself bandaging the arm of a young client who had cut herself. In a more serious crisis these pressures – to act rather than maintain a reflective stance – can become almost impossible to resist, as boundaries are attacked in various ways. Supervision becomes particularly important, to contain the anxiety of the therapist and help them think about the situation, rather than rushing into action. The supervisor also needs containment; part of this will come from internal resources, the theoretical underpinning which provides a framework for thought, the supervisor's experience and other personal qualities. But sometimes a supervisor will need to talk about their supervision session with their own supervisor or get support from others.

This chapter will focus mainly on the supervision of work with patients or clients in a crisis. We will also think further about difficulties or crises within the supervisory relationship.

Supervising work with patients in crisis: suicide and self harm

There are some settings where an actual suicide is an ongoing possibility; as Jeremy Holmes (1996) writes, 'most psychiatrists encounter suicide as an infrequent but unavoidable part of their work...For psychotherapists suicide is a much rarer and much more devastating experience' (p. 149). When it does happen, it causes enormous shock, grief and loss, as well having implication for relationships with colleagues and for the therapist's professional identity, as Jane Tillman (2006) documents in a study of analysts whose patients committed suicide. Because we know that such an experience would be devastating, probably the worst thing that could happen in one's professional life, the anxiety caused by a suicidal patient can be overwhelming, even if as many writers point out, actual suicide is rare compared with the number of clients in all settings who present with suicidal ideation.

Ann Heyno (2008), writing of this issue as it relates to the student population, considers what might lie behind this focus on actual versus potential suicide. Because a suicide attracts so much media attention, as well as blame, the very thought of it tends to induce a sense of panic which makes it difficult to consider suicide risk in a more thoughtful way. As she (p. 177) writes,

> Confusing actual death by suicide with suicidal thoughts gets in the way of thinking about what can be done to help the many students who feel suicidal. It also creates a situation in which omnipotence and denial are used as defences against the realistic anxiety that there are always some students who are at risk of killing themselves.

In common with a number of writers, she draws attention to the strength of the therapist's countertransference in this situation. If counsellors working with suicidal students can bear to receive and process the intense feelings involved in working with them, the risk of actual suicide is lessened; as she puts it, the counsellor needs to be 'affected without being infected' – that is, they need to allow themselves to take in the seriousness of the situation without becoming overwhelmed by it (p. 181). Heyno stresses the importance of sustained non judgemental support in supervision if this is to be achieved.

Joscelyn Richards (2007) also writes of reactions that can paralyse thinking – panic and helplessness, anger with the patient, worries about being blamed and a pressure to act rather than think (pp. 166–167). In addition there are more complex reactions, to do with colluding in some way with the patient, by failing to realise the seriousness of the situation, or explore suicidal thoughts in depth. Richards points out that, in confiding in the therapist, the sane part of the patient has placed a great deal of trust in them, and it is very important that the patient's despair, anger and desire to die are taken seriously. She gives a detailed and moving clinical example of a patient who attempted to get her to agree with him that he would be better off dead; in working with him she experienced very strong feelings, to do with being coerced and tortured, and recognised that she was being put in touch with the way in which her patient was tortured by the voices in his head that told him he had to die.

Richards stresses the importance of the role of the supervisor in exploring and helping to contain these countertransference feelings. This is vital, as we know that if the client or patient is able to talk with their therapist about their suicidal feelings and have them taken seriously, it can lessen the risk of their being acted out. This has a number of implications for supervision, since it can be very difficult to explore suicidal thoughts and feelings with patients if there is no sense of inner containment, fostered by good supervision.

We can identify a number of aspects to this containment:

- Allowing the supervisee to talk about the fears and feelings engendered by the session, and thinking about how the countertransference is related to what is going on with the patient or client.
- Thinking about the dynamics of the case with the supervisee, in terms of the unconscious purpose of suicide, for the patient.
- Helping the supervisee assess how serious the threat is.
- Thinking with the supervisee about ways of managing the situation. In some cases it may be enough to listen; at other times more direct action might be needed, in terms of the supervisee adopting a more managerial stance with the patient or by contacting mental health professionals who are able to intervene more directly.

Supervisors need to make clear the extent of their availability outside supervision times, particularly if they are clinically responsible for the work. In certain circumstances, this may include thinking about cover over holiday periods. I think it is important to let new supervisees know that they can make contact (telephone or e-mail) in an emergency; I have found that in practice this kind of contact is not needed very often. (Of course it is important not to be unrealistic about the extent of one's actual availability.) I also know that I have benefitted myself from having been able to talk to a supervisor in this kind of emergency. But I can also remember feeling strengthened by one supervisor's comment, once the immediate crisis had passed, that in similar circumstances in the future I would have the resources to manage the situation without contacting her. Supervisors have to judge the level of support the supervisee needs, allowing them to develop their own capacities for managing suicidal patients while helping them contain their anxieties.

Taking these supervisory tasks in turn, we have already mentioned the importance of processing the supervisee's thoughts and feelings about the session. This initially has a supportive function, but of course all countertransference reactions provide information about the client's or patient's state of mind. As we have seen in Chapter 5, the strength of such feelings may indicate the seriousness of the situation; we also saw that we need to listen for what is **not** being said, and not being picked up by the supervisee. As Campbell and Hale (1991) indicate in their very comprehensive chapter on suicidal acts, one of the warning signs for suicide can be a move towards a withdrawn passive state of mind which may result in a lessening of appropriate anxiety in those they are working with; the underlying anxieties are covered up, sometimes by an apparently more sanguine attitude. Bell (2001, p. 22) also states, 'dissociation is a more sinister sign than overt misery and depression.'

Anya, who was being seen in a university counselling service, did not seem to pose any kind of risk; although she had initially seemed depressed, the main theme of her recent sessions was her difficulty in getting her parents to understand her point of view. Mary, her counsellor, found she tended to lose focus when Anya started on this subject. She was very shocked therefore when, after a vacation break, extended by a missed session, Anya returned to counselling saying quite calmly that she had been in hospital since Mary had seen her last. She had taken an overdose – not an enormous one, but she had told a friend who had taken her to hospital ... She hadn't known whether to come back to counselling.

Mary tried to explore this further. The details were very hard to elicit but some incident at home, to do with one of her sisters, had seemed at the time quite intolerable. The really worrying thing, from Mary's point of view, was that Anya had no clear memory of how she had felt at the time of the overdose. When she woke up in hospital, she had felt euphoric, as though everything would be ok now. The only problem was, her parents had been very angry. They made her promise never to do this again, and hadn't spoken of the matter since. Anya also felt that she didn't want to go over it – which was why she thought she might not return to talk with Mary.

Mary's countertransference in recent sessions – which had often been to do with a sense of boredom, of feeling switched off – had failed to alert her to the potential seriousness of the situation, because Anya's anger and rage was also denied; she had talked of her frustration but the manner in which she told of her complaints gave the impression that there was nothing serious to worry about. Mary felt overwhelmed by guilt – she had clearly missed something. She felt as if her capacity to think had been lost.

In thinking about the dynamics of the case in supervision, they considered the likelihood that, in the break, Mary had become identified with an uncaring parental object who would choose to ignore her distress and react punitively if it was expressed. The supervisor was reminded of the need to stay alert and look beneath the surface of apparently bland material (of course this applied to the supervision as well as to the counselling). Anya was clearly very angry with both her parents. She was also furious with Mary at being abandoned, and in despair of anyone realising the seriousness of the situation. Her overdose acted as a warning and represented an act of revenge as far as her parents were concerned but also showed the turning in of this anger onto herself. The supervisor suggested that this needed to be put to Anya.

Situations where clients are at risk in any way test the supervisor's capacities in a number of ways. Our ability to keep calm and help our supervisees will depend partly on the way in which we have integrated our own theoretical understanding to think about the underlying dynamics, to do with unconscious conflict. If we understand that suppressed feelings, particularly of anger, can be deflected from our patient's internal objects onto themselves, and something of the strength of these murderous feelings in particular circumstances, we can help our supervisees to clarify what is going on. Both Campbell and Hale (1991) and Bell (2001) address the complexities underlying the dynamics of the internal world of the suicidal patient. It is not only a matter of more destructive impulses; some suicide attempts may represent a futile but sincere desire to preserve good objects or repair damaged objects, by splitting off and attacking bad, destructive parts of the self. We need therefore to understand the powerful impulses involved in the (unconscious) compulsion to atone for phantasised actions and thoughts.

The concept of the negative therapeutic reaction can also throw light on the situation; supervisees can sometimes be surprised, for example, that an apparent improvement on the part of the patient or client can be accompanied by a enormous hostility towards them, resulting partly from an increased awareness of their dependence on the therapist.

In supervision it is useful to start with a thorough examination of the content of the session, and what this implies for the degree of seriousness of the threat. The supervisee needs to encourage the client to elaborate their ideas about suicide, the extent to which they have made a plan to die, and the nature of this; they need to know that their therapist can bear to listen. There needs to be a consideration too about the nature of the communication, overt or more subtle, and what is implied not only for the degree of risk but in relation to the transference. The therapist may have to be helped to tolerate being the one who bears the anxiety about the possibility of death, while the client feels greatly relieved at having evacuated some of the more disturbing feelings; in turn the supervisor will inevitably be the recipient of the supervisee's anxiety.

The question of the extent to which such dynamics are interpreted to the client is a matter for discussion in supervision; some people who are functioning at a borderline level (see below) may become very disturbed if their wishes are interpreted too quickly, because they are unable to distinguish an interpretation or comment from an instruction or a statement of the literal truth. Thus in some circumstances an acknowledgement by the counsellor that the client thinks death is the answer to their difficulties might seem like a command to very disturbed clients, unless it is accompanied by a clear indication that the counsellor is there to help the client think about the situation and if necessary to help keep them safe. The therapist needs to show that they take the possibility of suicide very seriously.

A further function of supervision when dealing with suicidal clients or patients is helping supervisees work out who else, if anyone, needs to be informed. In some cases recognition of the depth of despair might be containment enough- to suggest anything more might make the client think that the therapist cannot bear to hear such thoughts. We know that in the client's mind, a referral can seem like a rejection. On the other hand it is not realistic – and verges on omnipotence – to imagine that a client or patient at serious risk can be contained without medical backup. In these cases we will need to suggest to the supervisee that they contact the GP or other clinician responsible for providing medical care. Normally this would only happen with the client's permission, but in supervision we sometimes find ourselves helping think about more serious cases, where the degree of risk is such that the client should be informed that the GP will be contacted. There may be cases where immediate admission to hospital is needed.

Arranging appropriate medical cover can help therapists maintain their own boundaries in the sessions; it means that they can allow the GP or the psychiatrist to manage medical elements of the treatment while continuing to work with the client on helping them understand the suicidal impulses and other aspects of their life. N. Keval (2003) writes of the need for a structure having the function of a safety net which can take over when a patient is in crisis, and stresses the importance of the different professionals involved being able to think things through together to avoid the patient creating unhelpful splits. There can then be a sense of being looked after by a helpful parental couple – the therapist and the doctor or medical team. Patients may of course refuse to allow this helpful communication to take place. In this event, the supervisor may need to help the therapist move to a more positive management of the situation.

The role of the supervisor in setting limits

A supervision group considered the case of a client being seen by the counselling service at a teaching hospital. Freda, a nursing student, had a history of long-standing difficulties – there was a mixture of suicidal thoughts, self harm and risk taking, together with an impulsiveness which made her counsellor very concerned for her long-term safety. Freda was attending appointments with the counsellor but was refusing to contact her GP or to allow the counsellor to do so, apparently because she thought her future on the course would be in jeopardy if the college authorities knew of the extent of her difficulties. When they talked about it in the group, it emerged that the counsellor didn't think there was an immediate risk, it was more that she felt she was being pressured into providing counselling without proper medical cover; she felt exposed, vulnerable and manipulated. But there was also a clear sense that in some way this young woman was 'special'; the counsellor felt that she was the only one that Freda trusted.

Since this situation had gone on for some weeks, the supervisor suggested that the counsellor should tell Freda that she would not be seen by the service again until she had been to the GP. The counsellor was clearly worried about letting Freda know about this, but eventually agreed, with some relief. The two others in the group disagreed with this course of action and voiced their concern that this very disturbed woman might be prevented from getting the help she needed by what they clearly saw as a rigid, rule-bound attitude on the part of the supervisor.

The supervisor – who had not been supervising the group for long – had found it difficult at first to use her authority. She maintained her stance however, while suggesting other ways that Freda might get treatment; in any case she considered that psychodynamic counselling, particularly without medical backup, was not the most suitable form of treatment for her at the moment. In the event Freda eventually got more appropriate help after a crisis visit to Accident and Emergency, but not before two other counselling services had told her that they could not take her.

In this case, the supervisor's views initially ran counter to those of her supervisees. We have already considered the way in which disagreements and polarised viewpoints can develop among professionals working with very ill patients. Tom Main writes vividly about this in his classic paper 'The ailment' (1957); certain patients seemed to create an 'in group' of over involved, attentive professionals while their colleagues, not favoured by the patient, made up an 'out group' who tended to be critical and unsympathetic towards the patient. These splits represent the way that such patients often think of themselves. Their behaviour, rooted in a need to exert an omnipotent control over their objects, as well as communicate the extent of their distress, can lead to disillusionment and burnout among those working with them. Main was writing about an in patient ward, but these dynamics show themselves in a more muted but still powerful form in many counselling agencies and out patient departments. The supervisor's ability to look clearly at the situation and if necessary make a firm suggestion is vital in these circumstances.

The following example relates to an attempted suicide and its ramifications within the institution in which it took place, and shows something of the way both the counsellor and the supervisor found themselves adopting a more active, consultancy role:

Margaret, an experienced counsellor, came to supervision very concerned about a student, Kasim, who had been found that morning on the college premises, barely conscious, by a caretaker; he had apparently taken an overdose and had been rushed to hospital.

Margaret had been seeing Kasim from time to time at the sixth form college where she worked, in connection with claustrophobic anxieties about attending his classes. He had a long history of very serious difficulties and was finding it hard to separate from his parents, feeling he had to conform to their expectations, but terrified of the implications of entry into the adult world. He had been a difficult student to get to know; while he had been both panicky and apparently anxious to get help, he was also paranoid and terrified of any closer involvement.

Margaret was preoccupied with two main issues; one was her own worry that she could have done more – had she been accessible enough? She had tried to get him to stick to his appointment times but it seemed as if he could not manage the sort of regular contact she was offering. She felt that others in the college might think she had failed to support him – certainly there had been various attempts by others having a welfare role in the college to get him to keep seeing Margaret, and it was clear that they felt overburdened by him – he kept turning up unexpectedly. She had seen him wandering around in the library near the counselling room earlier in the day, before he was discovered.

In supervision, they needed to spend some time processing the emotional impact of this event, Margaret's feeling of sadness but also of shock and guilt; she needed to feel she was supported in supervision. In actual fact, the supervisor felt that Margaret had done everything that could possibly be expected under the circumstances. She had brought this student several times to supervision as she had been very concerned about him, had contacted his GP with his permission and had recently managed to get him to see the psychiatrist at the local mental health centre. She had helped him explore his particular fears, and, the week before the overdose, had felt more optimistic that he could begin to think about his difficulties.

A further concern was the impact of this event on others in the institution, for example, the support that those involved in getting Kasim to hospital would need – they were clearly very shaken – and how the college might handle the situation.

In a later supervision the importance of having thought about these issues became clear. Margaret had had to put aside her purely counselling role and help the college management think about how to move forward, taking into account what was best for Kasim and what view the college should take if he wanted to return. The college authorities were in a dilemma – they did not want to be seen to exclude someone on mental health grounds and yet they were frightened that he would make *a second, successful attempt – they were all very concerned about him. The position was complicated by the fact that nothing more had been heard from Kasim, apart from the fact that the hospital confirmed he had been discharged.*

Margaret had to resist acting on an assumption that communicating with him or his family was the responsibility of the counsellor. In a sense Kasim's action had put his problems into a more public domain, and she needed to safeguard her own role as a counsellor in case he did return and wanted to talk with her. In supervision they had thought about his apparent need to both make contact and push people away, and the way he attended college but could not stay in the classes. It seemed as though the college had been functioning as some sort of container, almost like a day hospital, but problems had arisen when individuals expected him to engage with his teachers and his studies – this task was just beyond him at present, since he was far too ill.

The supervisor suggested that Margaret needed to keep these issues in mind, without necessarily spelling them out to the college authorities. She could however provide some useful psychodynamic insight into his state of mind. Margaret was able to make the point that Kasim would benefit from a clear and bounded attitude when it came to conditions for his return; her clinical judgement was that he would be relieved that he was not expected – or allowed – to return to a situation that had terrified him so much, and that the medical services needed to be asked for confirmation that he was fit to return. She was clear that the communication should be from the college administration.

The most difficult task for Margaret was to manage her own and other people's anxiety and frustration at not knowing the details of the outcome for Kasim; they would have liked reassurance about his health that she was not able to give and which she felt she could not ask for, for reasons of confidentiality.

Working with more disturbed clients

As these examples illustrate, the current scarcity of resources available to people with mental health difficulties means that often those with very severe difficulties present themselves for counselling or therapy in settings which are not well equipped to help them. This again requires the supervisor to help the supervisee think about the limits imposed by the setting, particularly where the supervisor has clinical responsibility for the work. But there are also limits relating to the level of experience of the supervisee, as well as the supervisor.

In Chapter 1 I suggested that supervisors need to have enough experience to have integrated aspects of theory and practice, and to be able to reflect psychodynamically on the client being presented without rushing defensively into a premature formulation of the problem. We may not always be responsible for assessing or allocating the clients or patients that our supervisees work with but we do need to be able to make some judgement about the client's level of disturbance and talk with our supervisee about the implications of this. While our supervisees will not necessarily be working in settings where clients are overtly psychotic, they will meet with many that would be clinically diagnosed as borderline or narcissistic as opposed to neurotic, and being able to indicate this is important in supervision. Theoretically we might think of these clients as functioning most of the time in the paranoid – schizoid position, implying, for example, that they will have a polarised way of looking at things, that their thinking may be on a concrete level and that in the case of more severely borderline patients or clients they may have a tendency to show their feelings by actions rather than words. Relationships, including that with the counsellor or psychotherapist will be difficult, because their experience of their internal objects is that they are difficult or unreliable in various ways.

Laurence Spurling (2003), in his paper on working with borderline clients, writes of the tremendous pressure that such people put on the counsellor, in terms of the intensity of the countertransference. The strength of these feelings is in itself an indication that the client is unable to symbolise; the distinction between fantasy and reality is lost. This might be an element in the example we considered in Chapter 5, where the therapist, Anita, found herself using an interpretation in a retaliatory way, with a patient with whom it was very difficult to make contact. While Anita's interpretation was clearly an enactment of her own frustration, it is also possible that the patient was in a state of mind where nothing that was said could be taken in, so that a comment would be experienced as an attack in a very concrete way. But this example also shows how easy it is for the therapist to get drawn into a concrete way of relating to the patient, where she too had to evacuate a thought rather than contain it, partly because she felt she just had to get through to him somehow. This kind of dynamic is also very likely to be evident when supervising those working in forensic settings; for a very powerful account of the vicissitudes of the transference under these circumstances, see Dorothy Lloyd-Owen's (1997) paper on this subject. The point is made that it is very easy under these circumstances for the supervisor to get drawn in also, into representing a punitive superego rather than enabling a more reflective stance to develop.

In this situation, one of the supervisor's main tasks is to support the therapist in simply surviving the attacks on the thinking and the work, without retaliating, so that there is a possibility of the relationship becoming less disturbing to the client. Another is to think with the counsellor about ways of framing interventions so that something can be taken in; there is a need for clarity and it may help to move to a more 'analyst-centred' way of making interventions (see Steiner (1993)) that allows the client to feel that they are being understood. Steiner points out that patients who are in a paranoid schizoid mode of thinking are not interested in gaining understanding, hence interpretations that centre on the patient seem like an attack. Helping our supervisees understand what is going on so that their interventions convey an empathetic understanding of the patient's state of mind is an important task of supervision.

A further task of supervision is to help the therapist think about and manage the volatile and unpredictable behaviour that can be a feature of working with such clients or patients. The supervisor also has to take into account what the supervisee can tolerate and the safety and other features of the setting.

Erica's client, Mr Z, had referred himself to a community counselling service because of his fears that his violence was getting out of control. After about six months of sessions, he developed a pattern of storming out of the consulting room, usually after an uneasy period of silence. Neither the supervisor nor Erica was sure what this meant; Erica said she did not feel under threat, but that she did feel immobilized. It was difficult to think how to address this. Erica said that it was hard not to get up and follow him, as she could hear him moving about outside the room, sometimes conveying a sense of anger and frustration with a sharp kick to the consulting room door. What Erica had been doing was simply staying in the room until the end of the session – she had discovered that Mr Z would always appear at this time, having stayed in the waiting area in the meantime. He would apologize and say, through gritted teeth, something along the lines of 'you know I would stay if I could'. Erica would simply say that she would see him next week.

Initially the supervisor tried to get Erica to make some kind of interpretation, with the aim of keeping him in the room, but Erica said she had a strong sense that this would not help, so they both decided to be patient. This was possible because of the idea that they both had, that Mr Z was not an actual threat to Erica, but was more frightened himself (saying this to Mr Z did seem to strike a chord). The supervisor also pointed out that, although it was a very concrete way of showing his feelings, kicking the door was not the same as kicking the counsellor. Erica was also worried about her colleagues being disturbed, although she realised that their presence in adjoining offices gave her a measure of additional protection.

*Some time later, long after Mr Z had stopped leaving the sessions in this manner, he was able to talk about it. He had been frightened of his fantasies about trashing Erica's room and, sometimes, of shouting at Erica; leaving the room was a way of protecting her, at a point when he was struggling with the difficulty of not acting out his thoughts. What he had really appreciated was Erica's staying there in the room, and being there at the end of the sessions; he could see that **she** could manage the situation, unlike other figures in his life, who had tended to retaliate.*

This example poses a number of questions about where to draw the line, in terms of whether a particular client can be seen in ordinary counselling settings. The supervisor might have been less happy about someone working with a client like Mr Z if they had been in a more isolated setting – in private practice for example. The fact that Erica had already built up an alliance with the client and that her countertransference suggested she need not be afraid was also taken into account, as was her level of experience. There was also a sense that Mr Z had a great many strengths and resources, although some deep-seated difficulties were coming to the surface. Both the supervisor and the counsellor thought that he was using the counselling in a very positive way, to make links between thought and action. But this sort of situation clearly poses dilemmas for the supervisor, depending as it does on an evaluation being made as to the actual safety of the counsellor. If there is any real doubt about this, and features of the setting mean that the therapist is working in isolation, then the work will have to be terminated and a more suitable referral made. Where the position is less clear or the counsellor is apprehensive, it helps to ensure that a colleague is within earshot and that appointments are made well within normal working hours. (The knowledge that there are others in the vicinity is containing to the client as well as the counsellor).

Difficulties within the supervisory relationship

Sometimes, dilemmas in supervision relate to the supervisee or to a problematic relationship between the supervisor and supervisee. As we have already seen, enactments and concrete thinking are not confined to our patients or clients. There are a number of circumstances that come to mind as having the potential to cause problems and difficulties. Sometimes these relate to idealised transferences on both sides. We may have misjudged the level of experience of our supervisees or the way in which they have used their training. We may discover, unexpectedly, that there are features of the way they work which cause us anxiety. Some of these may be due to different attitudes towards the boundaries of the work, perhaps stemming from unconsidered differences in theoretical orientation or training. Sometimes we may be concerned that our supervisees have embarked on a career for which they are not really suited, or that may be damaging their own emotional health.

These issues interact with our own tendencies and intolerances, and it is important to know where we stand when we begin supervising someone, to the extent that this is possible. Lou Corner (2007), writing of beginning supervision, stresses the need to have in our mind an idea of whom we are prepared to work with, based on our own experience and views. She suggests criteria that might be considered, including the question of training, theoretical orientation and level of experience, and the setting in which the supervisee works. She considers the ethical dimension, and our responsibility to create an atmosphere in which learning can take place. If we cannot respect aspects of the supervisee's work and other characteristics, it is better that we suggest they find another supervisor.

When we begin working with clients or patients it takes some time to build up an idea of our own boundaries in terms of who we will accept into our private practice or in other settings, and who we can work with. I think the same is true of supervision; we initially may take on supervisees that we may not be able to help in the long term, or we may have a somewhat omnipotent idea of the extent of the change that can take place in someone's work or attitude.

Different theoretical frameworks

The question of differing theoretical orientation comes to mind immediately as a possible obstacle to good supervision; readers will be clear by now that when we consider psychodynamic theory in the context of this book we are thinking of theories based primarily on psychoanalytic ideas. Looking at unconscious motivations and conflicts allows a consideration of the negative to be brought into focus in our work. In addition, the use of the concept of transference allows difficult ideas to be explored, potentially, in a somewhat less emotionally charged way – there is (often) an acceptance of the 'as if' quality of what transpires in a session. Therapists working in other modes where there is an emphasis on maintaining a positive alliance with the patient may find some psychoanalytic approaches unbearably cold and clinical, or the idea of the negative transference may not sit well with their beliefs about therapy. However we cannot make rules about this; often those coming with different theoretical orientations greatly value a psychodynamic framework. Their approach may have more similarities to our own way of looking at the work than we might have thought, which is useful learning for the supervisor.

Equally, there are various ways of conceptualising problems within a psychoanalytic frame. For example, there is a contrast between theories which focus on unconscious conflicts as a source of disturbance and those that consider aspects of deprivation as being more important in the early life of patients; ideas about the source of difficulties will influence the way in which we suggest interventions might be made. It is also true that our choice of theoretical approach – or the way we conceptualise and use it in thinking about our practice – is related to our own experience and identity. We also have to recognise that different levels of experience may influence the particular theories we espouse (see below).

Sometimes, other factors such as temperamental differences or attitudes to authority might be as important as differences in theoretical orientation, which may be brought into service as a rationale for conflict when there are other reasons for disagreement. In Chapter 3 I gave the example of Robert and his supervisee, John, where issues to do with rivalry and authority quickly developed as a feature of their relationship, and reflected anxiety on both sides. Here these issues are re-enacted in a further piece of work:

John brought his work with his client Sarah; it was clear that he took a rather literal view of Sarah's troubles, as being related to external events, and that he found it difficult to think about the transference, as well as revealing less about the actual content of the sessions than Robert would have liked. Robert put some of this down to inexperience; he thought, or perhaps hoped, that a good alliance had been built up between the therapeutic couple.

*As time went on, Robert found himself getting concerned that Sarah was apparently developing a very idealised transference to John. He was not challenging this, and seemed to be accepting a great deal of what she said at face value. In John's view, he was the one who **did** understand her, in contrast to the figures in the rest of her life, and in her past. He felt the important thing was to allow her the space to talk about and come to terms with what he clearly regarded as an emotionally bruising life experience.*

Robert considered that Sarah's material showed a much more angry side, which John was unable to see; he saw Sarah as using figures in her life as vehicles for projective identification, so that angry and aggressive feelings were experienced as existing in others, currently her manager at work. But he also became increasingly concerned about what he saw as John's over identification with his client, to the point where he seemed almost out of touch with psychic reality. John on the other hand felt quite invaded by Robert's demands to interpret the more destructive side of Sarah's behaviour. He didn't think it applied to the situation and accused Robert of being overbearing, and perhaps envious of the work he was doing with Sarah.

As the work went on, the disagreements continued and Robert noted a tendency for both of them to put it on to an apparently more intellectual plane. It became somewhat like a duel; the protagonists lined up their supporters, with John citing Winnicott and Robert feeling pressured into retaliating with some post-Kleinian theory.

Supervisors have to be prepared for challenges and disagreements about approaches to the work; that is part of the process. Earlier in this book (Chapters 4 and 5) I mentioned the role that our own unrecognised theories may play in our therapeutic work, but in addition there are more conscious identifications being made with particular theorists, sometimes represented by the persons of our teachers or analysts. Spurling (2003), in a paper on psychoanalytic figures as transference objects, considers this subject, and the way in which our own identifications and allegiances may change over time as we find that our existing theories are challenged by aspects of our clinical experience. This may be a factor in the disagreement between Robert and John, in the above example. But it seems likely that other more destructive forces are at work in the supervision sessions. As we have seen (Chapter 5) it is very common for supervisees to develop, temporarily, an idealised view of their relationship with their client. It seems as if John's idealisation had led to a rather punitive attitude in Robert, where the client and her inner world have got lost. John is finding it hard to value Robert's contribution, and their rivalry gets in the way of working together.

If there are serious, ongoing issues or disagreements within the supervisory framework these should be addressed; the question of whether someone may be better off with another supervisor may have to be considered. In addition, there might at times be real concerns about clients or patients being used unconsciously by the supervisee for their own emotional ends, and this has to be recognised and articulated to the supervisee.

Concerns about boundaries

Chapter 2 on beginning supervision stressed the importance of maintaining a bounded approach to supervision; this is particularly important for supervisees who have not yet internalised a knowledge of the importance of a bounded setting in their own work. Heather Wood (2007), writing of boundaries and confidentiality in supervision, reminds us how important it is to take into account the level of experience and professional maturity of our supervisees; while some of them will be more like professional colleagues others may require the care and attention to boundaries that we would give to work with patients. I would agree with her comment (p. 28) that mistakes in supervision often occur when we misjudge the extent to which our supervisees have absorbed a professional attitude to their work. We may find ourselves jolted and alarmed by revelations about work with clients, where there seems to be a haphazard attitude to endings, session times and other details of the frame. There are settings where boundaries might have to be less rigid, but it is disconcerting to discover that an apparently experienced supervisee had not thought about the implications of such conditions. As Wood points out (p. 25), it is easy, under these circumstances, for supervisors to become anxious and to overplay the monitoring aspect of supervision, emphasising rules rather than the need to think things through. This of course creates tensions for the supervisee, which may escalate if they cannot be thought about.

Psychotherapists, counsellors and supervisors are normally members of professional associations that have their own codes of ethics. Although there is not the space here to consider this matter in any detail, much of their content tends to deal with the idea of creating a bounded setting for therapeutic work. As supervisors we also need to be able to discriminate between situations where we can be more informal and those where we may need to model a more bounded approach.

Other boundary issues relate to the setting in which supervisees may work. In previous chapters we have often focussed on supervising work in institutions. I think that it is often more difficult to supervise those working in private practice, partly because it may take some while to get a sense of the setting in which the work takes place. It is necessary to be aware of features relating to this setting, as well as to how the practitioner relates to sources of referral and support networks, and the constraints and opportunities of their working environment.

In private practice, therapists may be taking on clients and patients who have got their name through directories or advertisements or their own web site; under these circumstances a thorough assessment is essential. The supervisor can help the supervisee think about what constitutes a good assessment; as always, such an assessment needs to take into account the context of the work as well as discovering something about the client or patient and the seriousness of the issues or degree of disturbance. There also needs to be some thinking in supervision about the kind of support systems that are useful for counsellors in private practice, to safeguard the client as well as the practitioner; some supervisors would suggest that the client's GP should always be contacted for example, but in any case the degree to which the supervisor finds themselves getting involved in thinking about these issues must depend on the level of experience of the supervisee and whether they think there are concerns about any aspects of practice.

Newly qualified counsellors can find private practice to be a very difficult setting (and it may be best left until people have more experience in other settings) partly because the therapist may be working in comparative isolation. Maintaining boundaries of all kinds can become more problematic; distinctions between personal and professional life have to be thought about if the counsellor is working at home, and there is less opportunity for informal contact and discussion with colleagues when small dilemmas present themselves. In supervision we need to be aware of these pressures, and supervision may have to provide an extra level of containment, as well as challenging ways of working that show an inattention to boundaries.

Supporting supervisees and ourselves

From time to time supervisees and supervisors will have difficulties in their lives which need thinking about in relation to supervision; I am thinking here of problems such as bereavements, illness, family problems or other factors that may require time off work. Most codes of practice or ethics stress the need for practitioners to take responsibility for monitoring their own well-being and taking appropriate measures to safeguard this and that of their patients. Supervisors faced with a supervisee in a personal crisis need to think about the containment they are offering, to think through the situation realistically, and make firm suggestions if they feel that the supervisee is not in a position to think clearly. Sometimes we may have to suggest that the supervisee takes a break from clinical work. In addition it is important that any practitioner working independently has a system in place whereby a colleague has the responsibility of contacting patients in an emergency; this naturally applies to supervisors as well as supervisees.

Much of this chapter has focused on situations where the patients' situations have contributed towards uncertainties and dilemmas. But we have also briefly thought about challenges within the supervisory relationship. Sometimes, as is the case with patients, we cannot foresee difficulties – and it is in the nature of a crisis that it cannot be planned for in any detail. Putting systems in place to deal with more likely events is helpful. Anyone who has ever had to face the possibility of suddenly having to stop therapeutic work will appreciate the importance of having up-to-date information about patient contact details readily to hand, and someone to take responsibility for contacting them. When we are faced with events that we cannot foresee, we have to fall back on our ability to provide and maintain a space for thinking things through. Our own supervision or other support is very important in these circumstances.

Summary and conclusions

In this chapter we have considered situations that pose particular challenges in supervision. We have focused in particular on the suicidal patient as well as those presenting with other serious difficulties, and noted the way in which the levels of anxiety engendered by working with this patient group make it particularly difficult to allow a thoughtful assessment of the situation. The supervisor has the dual role of maintaining this reflective space, and keeping in mind the boundaries of therapeutic work but also of helping the supervisee think about appropriate actions where patients are in a life-threatening situation. The kind of challenges and crises we are considering in this chapter are an extreme instance of these dilemmas.

Difficulties relating to the supervisory relationship itself are also discussed; many of these stem from the supervisor misjudging the level of experience or sophistication of the supervisee. Others have their origins in the personal and emotional dynamics that we have considered earlier in the book. Finally we consider briefly the need for supervisors to have their own sources of support.

In conclusion:

- The types of serious crises we have considered in this chapter put additional pressures on supervision. Because of the anxiety generated, the supervisee can feel pulled into taking up a more active stance when the patient or client is perceived to be at risk, and the supervisor in turn is under great pressure to be more active, in terms of making suggestions for interventions. There is a paradox, in that a more active supervisory stance may well be appropriate in an emergency, but at the same time the situation calls for thoughtful containment and the preservation of a space to think.
- We need to be aware of the particular sorts of pressures that patients or clients who are at risk put on the supervisee, and the way we may experience these in the countertransference. Sometimes the effect of the patient on the supervisee may be to numb them, destroying the capacity to think or to realise how serious the situation might be. Patients experiencing crises may be very uncertain of their own state of mind and this is sometimes reflected in different or opposing views being taken by the supervisor and the supervisee.
- The supervisor has to provide the containment to allow the supervisee to experience the difficult and sometimes destructive feelings generated in the session without retaliation. Being able to survive such feelings is very important therapeutically – of course this also applies in supervision. But where patients have a tendency to enact their feelings physically rather than by being verbally aggressive, we also have to be mindful of the safety of the supervisee.
- Difficulties in the supervisory relationship can also put great pressures on the supervisor, and need to be thought about if they are getting in the way of working together to think about the patient.

Such situations are less likely to occur if both parties are conscious of their expectations about the different aspects of supervision at the beginning of the relationship.

- What all of these situations have in common is their tendency to generate strong feelings, which need to be processed before being acted upon. Nevertheless, faced with such crises, the supervisor may well need to move to a more managerial, monitoring mode of working.
- Finally, if we are to provide containment and support in crises, we need to develop resources of help and support for ourselves.

CONCLUSION

In the course of writing this book, a number of themes have stayed in my mind, and this very brief section draws together some of these ideas. The first chapter posed the question of what it is that makes supervision such a difficult task at times. A large part of this is that, as we have seen, supervision requires an alertness to the way in which circumstances are changing and the ability to respond accordingly; it is a complex and dynamic process where rules and procedures may provide a guide but they cannot provide an answer.

We have thought about the role of boundaries of various kinds. There is a need to provide, as far as possible, a consistent space for supervision in terms of time and place and other features of the setting. We have seen that this is important in terms of providing a sense of containment for the supervisee but it is also important for the supervisor. Paying attention to this aspect of supervision is one of the many instances in which what we do in supervision is at times more important than what we say.

We have also thought about boundaries in terms of the possible tasks or functions of supervision – educative, monitoring, supporting and managing. How we think about these boundaries will affect the way we take up the role of supervisor but the lines cannot be fixed for all time. We need, when supervising, to find our own personal position but the balance is constantly shifting, taking into account our own assessment of what is the required focus. The different functions of supervision will become more or less predominant in different circumstances. This is part of the complexity of supervision; it requires a consistent attention and responsiveness to the needs of our individual supervisees as well as the safety of their patients, in the context in which they are working. The aim is to provide a setting in which these different aspects can be thought about. But not all the responsibility lies with the supervisor; as I suggest in the last paragraph of this conclusion, this is a joint enterprise.

This is an introductory book and there are areas that have not been covered – or not been covered in any detail. There are client or patient groups which have not been considered, in particular the area of supervising work with children and adolescents, and that of working with patients in forensic settings. Supervising brief therapy is another topic which I have not covered. I've written about complicated supervisory relationships but I have not covered the kind of supervisory crisis which results in a complaint or disciplinary action, affecting either supervisor or supervisee. Such cases are very idiosyncratic and I think it is important, apart from consulting one's own supervisor or professional colleagues, to make contact with the relevant professional body or ethics committee; there is plenty of help and advice available, suited to the individual circumstances.

Finally I want to emphasise something that is implicit throughout much of this book. As supervisors we cannot function without supervisees any more than we can be therapists if we have no patients. And the quality of the supervisory relationship is clearly important for good supervision. But for good supervision to take place, supervisees need to take responsibility for their part in the progress of the work of supervision. There needs to be an openness to learning and a preparedness to engage in what is, perhaps inevitably, a very exposing and anxiety-provoking process. The supervisor can facilitate the development of this state of mind, but its presence also requires determination and much hard work on the part of the supervisee. In the course of writing this book, I have been very aware of my own experience as a supervisee as well as a supervisor, and I think being able to draw on this experience, as supervisors, is important. I also hope that this book might be helpful for supervisees in thinking about the vicissitudes of the supervisory relationship and the part they play in making it more useful and productive.

Appendix: Sources of Information on Supervision

The contacts on this list may be a useful beginning for those wanting to find out more about supervision courses and organisations with a special interest in the subject.

A number of organisations run courses on supervision from a psychodynamic perspective. Their web sites will have up-to-date information.

- British Association of Psychotherapists (www.bap-psychotherapy.org)
- Guild of Psychotherapists (www.guildofpsychotherapists.org.uk)
- Society of Analytical Psychology (www.thesap.org.uk)
- WPF therapy (www.wpf.org.uk)

In addition the BAP runs a supervision service for psychotherapists and counsellors wanting to find a psychoanalytically orientated supervisor.

The British Association for Psychoanalytic and Psychodynamic Supervision (www.supervision.org.uk) brings together psychotherapists and accredited counsellors with a particular interest and training in supervision. They have a written code of ethics to which all members subscribe, publish a newsletter and organise conferences relating to supervision several times a year.

The British Association for Counselling and Psychotherapy (www.bacp.co.uk) have a scheme for accrediting supervisors and also have a written code of ethics on supervision. In addition they publish information on training courses on supervision.

REFERENCES

Alleyne, A. (August 2005). 'Invisible injuries and silent witnesses: The shadow of racial oppression in workplace contexts.' *Psychodynamic Practice* 11(3): 283–299.

Armstrong, D. (2005). 'Organization in the mind: An introduction.' *Organization in the Mind*. London: H. Karnac.

Arundale, J. (2007). 'Supervising trainees: Teaching the values and techniques of psychoanalytic psychotherapy' in Petts, A. and Shapley, B. (eds) *On Supervision: Psychoanalytic and Jungian Perspectives*. London: H. Karnac.

Bell, D. (2001). 'Who is killing what or whom? Some notes on the internal phenomenology of suicide.' *Psychoanalytic Psychotherapy* 15(1): 21–37.

Berman, E. (2000). 'Psychoanalytic supervision: The inter-subjective development.' *International Journal of Psychoanalysis* 81, Part 2: 273–290.

Bion, W.R. (1961). *Experiences in Groups*. London: Routledge, 1989.

——. (1962). 'A theory of thinking.' *Second Thoughts*, pp. 110–119. London: H. Karnac, 1984.

——. (1979). 'Making the best of a bad job.' Unpublished lecture to the British Psychoanalytical Society, quoted in Symington, N. (1986) *The Analytic Experience*. London: Free Association Books.

Bollas, C. (2000). *Hysteria*. London and New York: Routledge.

Brown, L. and Miller, M. (2002). 'The triadic intersubjective matrix in supervision.' *International Journal of Psychoanalysis* 83, Part 4: 811–824.

Campbell, D. and Hale, R. (1991). Chapter 12 'Suicidal acts' in Holmes, J. (ed.) *A Textbook of Psychotherapy in Psychiatric Practice*. London: Churchill Livingstone.

Caper, R. (1999). *A Mind of One's Own*. New Library of Psychoanalysis, London: Routledge.

Casement, P. (1985). *On Learning from the Patient*. London: Routledge.

——. (1990). *Further Learning from the Patient*. London: Tavistock/Routledge.

Cohen, M. (2003). *Sent Before My Time: A Child Psychotherapist's View of Life on a Neonatal Intensive Care Unit*. London: H. Karnac.

Coleman, W. (2006). 'The analytic superego.' *The Journal of the British Association of Psychotherapists* 44(2): 99–114.

Coren, A. (1997). *A Psychodynamic Approach to Education*. London: Sheldon Press.

——. (2001). *Short-Term Psychotherapy: A Psychodynamic Approach*. Basingstoke: Palgrave Macmillan.

Corner, L. (2007). Chapter 1 'On beginning a supervisory relationship' in Petts, A. and Shapley, B. (eds) *On Supervision: Psychoanalytic and Jungian Perspectives*. London: H. Karnac.

Crick, P. (1991). 'Good supervision: On the experience of being supervised.' *Psychoanalytic Psychotherapy* 5(3): 235–245.

Dalal, F. (1998). *Taking the Group Seriously.* London and Philadelphia: Jessica Kingsley Publishers.

———. (2002). *Race, Colour and the Processes of Racialization.* Hove: Brunner-Routledge.

Davids, M. Fakhry (May 2003). 'The internal racist.' *Bulletin of the British Psychoanalytical Society* 39(4): 1–15.

Del Pozo, M.M. (1997). Chapter 2 'On the process of supervision in psychoanalytic psychotherapy' in Martindale et al. (eds) *Supervision and Its Vicissitudes*, EFPP Clinical Monograph Series. London: H. Karnac.

Freud, S. (1893–1895). 'Fraulein Elisabeth von R' in Breuer, J. and Freud, S. (eds) *Studies on Hysteria*, S.E. II. London: Hogarth Press, 1955.

———. (ed.) (1911). 'Formulations on the two principles of mental functioning' *Papers on Technique*, S.E. XII. London: Hogarth Press, 1958.

———. (ed.) (1913). 'On beginning the treatment' *Papers on Technique*, S.E. XII. London: Hogarth Press, 1958.

———. (1914a). 'Remembering, repeating and working through', S.E. XII, pp. 145–156. London: Hogarth Press and the Institute of Psychoanalysis, 1955.

———. (1914b). 'Some reflections on schoolboy psychology', S.E. XIII, pp. 241–244. London: Hogarth Press and the Institute of Psychoanalysis, 1955.

———. (1921). *Group Psychology and the Analysis of the Ego*, S.E. XVIII. London: Hogarth Press.

———. (ed.) (1933). 'Lecture 31: The dissection of the psychical personality.' *New Introductory Lectures on Psycho-Analysis and Other Works*, S.E. XXII. London: Hogarth Press, 1960.

Frosh, S. (1997). Chapter 7 'Psychoanalytic agendas: Gender, homosexuality and racism.' *For and Against Psychoanalysis*. London: Routledge.

Gordon, P. (May 1996). 'A fear of difference? Some reservations about intercultural therapy and counselling.' *Psychodynamic Counselling* 2(2): 195–208.

Gosling, R.H. (1981). 'A study of very small groups' in Grotstein, J.S. (ed.) *Do I Dare Disturb the Universe? A Memorial to W.R. Bion.* London: H. Karnac, 1983.

Gray, A. (1994). *An Introduction to the Therapeutic Frame.* London and New York: Routledge/Brunner-Routledge.

Halton, W. (1995). 'Institutional stress on providers in health and education.' *Psychodynamic Counselling* 1(2): 187–197.

Hartung, B.M. (1979). 'The capacity to enter latency in learning pastoral psychotherapy.' *Journal of Supervision and Training in Ministry (USA)* 2: 46–59.

Hawkins, P. and Shohet, R. (2000). *Supervision in the Helping Professions*, 2nd edition. Maidenhead: Open University Press.

Heimann, P. (1950). 'On counter-transference.' *International Journal of Psychoanalysis* 31: 81–84.

Heyno, A. (2008). Chapter 14 'On being affected without being infected: Managing suicidal thoughts in student counselling' in Briggs, S.,

Lemma, A., and Crouch, W. (eds) *Relating to Self-harm and Suicide*. London: Routledge.

Hinshelwood, R. and Skogstad, W. (2000). 'Reflections on health care cultures' in *Observing Organisations*. London: Routledge.

Holmes, J. (1996). Chapter 6 'Suicide and attachment theory' in *Attachment, Intimacy Autonomy*. Amsterdam: Jason Aronson.

Howard, S. (2007). 'Models of supervision' in Petts, A. and Shapley, B. (eds) *On Supervision: Psychoanalytic and Jungian Perspectives*. London: H. Karnac.

Ingram, G. (2003). 'Ending and the nature of therapeutic time: Examples from art, culture and brief therapy.' *Psychodynamic Practice* 9(4): 521–546.

Jacobs, M. (1996). 'Parallel process-confirmation and critique.' *Psychodynamic Counselling* 2(1): 55–66.

Jones, R. (1989). 'Supervision: A choice between equals?' *British Journal of Psychotherapy* 5(4): 505–511.

Joseph, B. (1982). 'On understanding and not understanding' in Feldman, M. and Bott Spillius, E. (eds) *Psychic Equilibrium and Psychic Change*. New Library of Psychoanalysis, London: Routledge, 1989.

——. (1983). 'Transference: The total situation' in Feldman, M. and Bott Spillius, E. (eds) *Psychic Equilibrium and Psychic Change*. New Library of Psychoanalysis, London and New York: Routledge, 1989.

Kareem, J. (November 1988). 'Outside in-inside out . . . some considerations in intercultural psycho-therapy.' *Journal of Social Work Practice* 3: 57–71.

Kernberg, O. (1996). 'Thirty methods to destroy the creativity of psychoanalytic candidates.' *International Journal of Psychoanalysis* 77: 1031–1040.

Keval, N. (2003). 'Triangulation or strangulation: Managing the suicidal patient.' *Psychoanalytic Psychotherapy* 17(1): 35–51.

Khan, M. Masud. (1972). 'The becoming of a psycho-analyst' in *The Privacy of the Self*. London: Hogarth Press, 1981.

Klein, M. (1935). 'A contribution to the psychogenesis of manic depressive states' in *Love, Guilt and Reparation and Other Works*. London: Virago Press, 1988.

——. (1959). 'Our adult world and its roots in infancy' in *Envy and Gratitude and Other Works 1946–1963*. London: Virago Press, 1988.

King, L. and Randall, R. (eds) (2003). *The Future of Psychoanalytic Psychotherapy*. London: Whurr Publishers.

Langs, R. (1979). *The Supervisory Experience*. London and New York: Jason Aronson.

Langs, R. (1994). *Doing Supervision and Being Supervised*. London: H. Karnac.

Lemma, A. (May 1999). 'Starting from scratch: Developing clinical psychology training and services in Bangladesh.' *Psychodynamic Counselling* 5(2): 193–204.

Lloyd-Owen, D. (1997). Chapter 6 'From action to thought: Supervising mental health workers with forensic patients' in Martindale et al. (ed.) *Supervision and Its Vicissitudes*. London: H. Karnac.

Lowe, F. (February 2008). 'Colonial object relations: Going underground Black–White relationships.' *British Journal of Psychotherapy* 24(1): 20–33.

Main, T. (1957). 'The Ailment' in *The Ailment and Other Psychoanalytic Essays*. London: Free Association Books, 1989.

Mattinson, J. (1975). *The Reflection Process in Casework Supervision*. London: Institute of Marital Studies, The Tavistock Institute of Human Relations.

McGlashan, R. (2003). 'The individuating supervisor' in Wiener, J., Mizen, R., and Duckham, J. (eds) *Supervising and Being Supervised*. Basingstoke: Palgrave Macmillan.

Menzies Lyth, I. (1960). 'Social systems as a defense against anxiety.' *The Social Engagement of Social Science, Volume 1*. London: Free Association Books, 1990.

Miller, E.J. and Rice, A.K. (1967). 'Selections from "Systems of Organization".' *Group Relations Reader 1*. Jupiter, FL: A.K. Rice Institute, 1975.

Milner, M. (1952). 'Aspects of symbolism and comprehension of the not-self.' *International Journal of Psychoanalysis* 33: 181–195.

Milton, J. (2001). 'Psychoanalysis and cognitive behaviour: Rival paradigms or common ground?' *International Journal of Psychoanalysis* 82, Part 3: 431–448.

Mollon, P. (1997). 'Supervision as a space for thinking' in Shipton, G. (ed.) *Supervision of Psychotherapy and Counselling: Making a Place to Think*. Buckingham: Open University Press.

Morgan, H. (1998). 'Between fear and blindness: The white therapist and the black patient.' *Journal of the British Association of Psychotherapists* 3(34), Part 1: 48–61.

——. (2007). 'The effects of "race" and colour in supervision' in Petts, A. and Shapley, B. (eds) *On Supervision: Psychoanalytic and Jungian Perspectives*. London: H. Karnac.

Ogden, T.H. (1982). *Projective Identification and Psychotherapeutic Technique*. London: H. Karnac.

——. (2005). 'On psychoanalytic supervision.' *International Journal of Psychoanalysis* 86, Part 5: 1265–1280.

Papadopoulos, R. (2002). 'But how can I help if I don't know? Supervising work with refugee families' in Campbell, D. and Mason, B. (eds) *Perspectives on Supervision*. London: H. Karnac.

Phillips, S.H. (2003). 'Homosexuality: Coming out of the confusion.' *International Journal of Psychoanalysis* 84: 1431–1450.

Racker, H. (1968). *Transference and Countertransference*. Reprinted. London: H. Karnac, 1982.

Richards, J. (2007). Chapter 10 'The role of supervision (internal and external) in working with the suicidal patient' in Petts, A. and Shapley, B. (eds) *On Supervision: Psychoanalytic and Jungian Perspectives*. London: H. Karnac.

Rioch, M. (1975). 'The work of Wilfred Bion on groups' in Colman, A.D. and Bexton, W.H. (eds) *Group Relations Reader 1*. Jupiter, FL: A.K Rice Institute.

Roberts, V.Z. (1994a). 'The organisation of work: Contributions from open systems theory' in Obholzer, A. and Roberts, V.Z. (eds) *The Unconscious at Work*. London: Routledge.

——. (1994b). 'The self-assigned impossible task' in Obholzer, A. and Roberts, V.Z. (eds) *The Unconscious at Work*. London: Routledge.

Rustin, M. (1991). *The Good Society and the Inner World*. London and New York: Verso.

Salzberger-Wittenberg, I. (1983). Chapter 1 'Hopeful, and fearful expectations' in Salzberger-Wittenberg, I., Henry, G., and Osborne, E. (eds) *The Emotional Experience of Learning and Teaching*. London: Routledge.

Scanlon, C. (2002). 'Group supervision of individual cases in the training of counsellors and psychotherapists: Towards a group analytic model?' *British Journal of Psychotherapy* 19(2): 219–233.

Schaverien, J. (2003). 'Supervising the erotic transference and countertransference' in Wiener, J., Mizen, R., and Duckham, J. (eds) *Supervising and Being Supervised*. Basingstoke: Palgrave Macmillan.

Searles, H.F. (1955). 'The informational value of the supervisor's emotional experiences' in *Collected Papers on Schizophrenia and Related Subjects*. London: Maresfield Library, 1965.

Segal, J. (May 1996). 'Whose disability? Countertransference in work with people with disabilities.' *Psychodynamic Counselling* 2(2): 155–166.

Solomon, H. (2007). Chapter 3 'The ethics of supervision: Developmental and archetypal perspectives' in Petts, A. and Shapley, B. (eds) *On Supervision: Psychoanalytic and Jungian Perspectives*. London: H. Karnac.

Spillius, E.B. (1992). 'Clinical experiences of projective identification' in Anderson, R. (ed.) *Clinical Lectures on Klein and Bion*. New Library of Psychoanalysis, London: Routledge.

Spurling, L. (February 2003). 'Transference with the borderline client: Some implications for training psychodynamic counsellors.' *Psychodynamic Practice* 9(1): 25–42.

——. (2003). 'On psychoanalytic figures as transference objects.' *International Journal of Psychoanalysis* 84, Part 1: 31–44.

——. (2004). *An Introduction to Psychodynamic Counselling*. Basingstoke: Palgrave Macmillan.

Steiner, J. (1992). 'The equilibrium between the paranoid-schizoid and the depressive position' in Anderson, R. (ed.) *Clinical Lectures on Klein and Bion*. New Library of Psychoanalysis, London: Routledge.

——. (1993). 'Problems of psychoanalytic technique: Patient-centred and analytst-centred interpretations' in *Psychic Retreats*. New library of Psychoanalysis, London and New York: Routledge.

——. (2006). 'Interpretative enactments and the analytic setting.' *International Journal of Psychoanalysis* 87, Part 2: 315–320.

Stewart, N. (2004). 'Supervising the primary care counsellor within the psychodynamic frame.' *Psychodynamic Practice* 10(3): 354–372.

Tan, R. (1993). 'Racism and similarity: Paranoid-Schizoid structures.' *British Journal of Psychotherapy* 10(1): 33–43.

Temperley, J. (1984). 'Our own worst enemies: Unconscious factors in female disadvantage.' *Free Associations* 1A: 23–38.

Terry, P. (2008). *Counselling and Psychotherapy with Older People*, 2nd edition. Basingstoke: Palgrave Macmillan.

Tillman, J.G. (2006). 'When a patient commits suicide: An empirical study of psychoanalytic clinicians.' *International Journal of Psychoanalysis* 87, Part 1: 159–178.

Timimi, S. (1996). 'Race and colour in internal and external reality.' *British Journal of Psychotherapy* 13(2): 183–192.

Tuckett, D. (2005). 'Does anything go? Towards a framework for the more transparent assessment of psychoanalytic competence.' *International Journal of Psychoanalysis* 86, Part 1: 31–50.

Twyman, M. (2007). 'Some dynamics of Supervision' in Petts, A. and Shapley, B. (eds) *On Supervision:Psychoanalytic and Jungian Perspectives.* London: H. Karnac.

Winnicott, D.W. (1941). 'The observation of infants in a set situation' in *Through Paediatrics to Psychoanalysis.* London: Hogarth Press, 1958.

——. (1947). 'Hate in the countertransference' in *Through Paediatrics to Psychoanalysis.* London: Hogarth Press.

——. (1962). 'The child in health and crisis' in *The Maturational Process and the Facilitating Environment.* London: The Institute of Psychoanalysis/ H. Karnac, 1965.

Wood, H. (2007). Chapter 2 'Boundaries and confidentiality in supervision' in *On Supervision: Psychoanalytic and Jungian Perspectives.* London: H. Karnac.

Zinkin, L. (1988). 'Supervision: The impossible profession'. British Association of Psychotherapists. Papers from a public conference, London.

INDEX

rivalry, 36–8, 71, 88–9
Roberts, V. Zagier, 115, 117
role of supervisee, 44, 147, 168–9
  in groups, 88
  of supervisor, 3–10, 34, 44, 109, 153
Rustin, M, 131

Salzberger-Wittenberg, I, 38, 40
Scanlon, C, 97
Schaverien, J, 140
Searles, H.F, 53–6
Segal, J, 143
setting, 19–22, 24, 29–30, 83, 116, 164
shame, 37, 105, 135
Solomon, H, 2, 5
Spillius, E. Bott, 53
splitting, 37, 95, 105, 112, 131–9, 151–4
  see also projective identification
Spurling, L, 11, 22, 157, 162
Steiner, J, 80, 91, 158
Stewart, N, 118
suicidal patients, 79, 148–56
superego influences, 43, 46, 134–5

Tan, R, 129–30, 131
tasks, of supervision, 24–9, 67–82,
  90–2
Temperley, J, 138
Terry, P, 111, 141–2

theory,
  function of, in supervision, 49,
    62–5
  group relations, 110–117
  groups, 89–98
  psychoanalytic, 10–11, 49–53
  of supervision, 53–62
  systems theory, 116–17
  implicit, 12, 62, 162
  integration of theory with practice, 16,
    62–3, 77
  see also parallel process
Tillman, J G, 148
Timimi, S, 131
transference, 73–80
  erotic, 100, 140–1
  in institutions, 123–4
  to learning, 36–9, 44–5
  in relation to difference, 129
  to supervisor, 44, 59–61
  see also countertransference
triangular space, 2, 79
Tuckett, D, 82–3
Twyman, M, 8

Winnicott. D.W, 19, 22, 27, 51
Wood, H, 163

Zinkin, L, 2